Trails
Dreams Events
Of
Lone Elk

By
Dale Lone Elk Casteel

Published by:
Bluewater Publications, LLC
1812 CR 111
Killen, Alabama 35645
www.BluewaterPublications.com

Edited by Mary Lou Hill

Acknowledgements

Thank you Mary Lou Hill for all the help given me to make this book happen. Without her it would not have come together. I am very grateful for all you have done.

Thank you to each of you who have purchased my books and continue to support me. Those who have all my books continue to ask me when I will have another one. I am very humbled that you would ask.

Thank You my God the Creator of all life. Without Him I could not have accomplished any of this. He is the one that put these ideas into my heart. My God, I thank You so much.

Other Books by Dale Lone Elk Casteel

The End of the Trail of Tears

The Trail That I Traveled

The Native People of Turtle Island

The Greatest Race

Great Words of Wisdom from the First Native People

My Prayer

O Great Spirit, teach me to heed the Word You have spoken.
Let me feel Your presence always within my heart.

Let the Wind bring the Message You would have my ears to Hear.
Be a Guiding light for me to See
The Pathway that You would have me travel.

Let me see Your Face in every Tree, in every Rock,
And in every Creature that walks this Earth
So that it will remind me of Your Great Works!

Let me travel in Your Shadow so that I will never lose sight of
Who You Are! Teach me to respect all Human Beings
And, all the animals that walk On This Earth.

Let my footprints be a Trail that I would have all my
Children follow when I bow down to pray or look to the
Heavens Let Your Face be the Face I look upon!

Give me Knowledge—not for what I desire, but to
Understand the things You want of me!
Let me show respect for my Elders
Give me Strength to face my enemies and
Compassion to Forgive!

Teach me to give back more than I take from Mother Earth
And, treat it for what it is—"Sacred Ground."

When my eyes grow dim and my body is frail and weary
And when my life begins to fade as the setting of the Sun,

Put this thought in my heart,
"It is a good day to go . . . Home"

Foreword

Many people have asked me to write another book. Some have asked me to make a book out of the many short stories and essays I have written. At the peoples' request I have decided to do that.

Many of my stories have some of the same information in them because I write a lot about the same subjects. I hope they will be something you will enjoy and try to understand where I am come from.

Being a firm believer in helping Native American Indians and their way of life, I believe this earth should be considered Sacred Ground to all people. All people should not be living off this land, but living within it.

In my view, the Indian people are becoming stronger each day even though there are many on reservations who still struggle to get by. One day this will change and yes, one day we will have a Native American Indian for President of the United States of America. I pray that this country can survive until that happens.

Table of Contents

Dedication

L-R Cruz, Nakota, Yvette, Huyanha and Sean Collin

This book is dedicated to a family that took me in and made me part of it. They named me Godfather to Nakota Braveheart and Grandpa to Huyanha and Cruz. Yvette and Sean I thank you. You put new life into this old man. I love each of you as my family.

Sacred Ground

In my life, I have traveled west a few times. On my last trip in 2000, I recall the highways being free from litter, the grass neatly groomed and the purity of the lakes, rivers and streams.

It was a joy to ride along clean highways free from garbage and it made me think about the folks that lived in the area and how they must really care about their state. Then, I began to ponder about my home and the slogan on the sign at the state line that reads—*Alabama the Beautiful.*

How I wish the sides of our highways and roadways were not full of litter. I wonder if people think we try to hide our litter by allowing the grass to grow tall along the roadsides and highways.

It is a disgrace to allow the junk and garbage to collect on the sides of our highways and roads. Are we a people that have no concern about the future? Do we realize that all this pollution will affect our children and grandchildren? Does it matter what visitors think about us when traveling through Alabama?

First impressions are lasting impressions and I wonder what impression our highways make on people who travel through our state. Certainly it would not leave a positive image about our state to anyone.

Our rivers, lakes and streams are even worse than our highways. Recently, I went fishing with a friend and was deeply saddened by the amount of garbage and junk that floated downstream, probably because the banks were already full of litter. It was a pitiful sight to behold. If one could get five cents for plastic bottles, then one could make a million dollars just along the banks of the Elk River alone.

Born and raised here, I love Alabama. It is unusual because to the South there is the ocean, to the North there are the great mountains and rolling hills, and the flat lands are in between. Water, a natural resource, is plentiful in this great state. It could almost be a picture perfect place to live or visit so why do we allow our waters to be contaminated, our air to be polluted and our highways to be littered?

As a child in North Alabama, I remember the rivers, lakes and streams being clean and beautiful. Back then it was the best thing this side of Heaven. The Tennessee Valley Authority hired a crew to clean the riverbanks of litter and burn the driftwood each fall. During that period of time, electric bills were two or three dollars a month. Supposedly our state can no longer afford to hire the crews but now our electric bills are two or three hundred dollars a month! This makes me wonder exactly how the money is used today. My childhood years are precious and I would not trade them for any other period of time. I was fortunate to have grown up during those times; the best times this country ever experienced.

The Bible tells us that God made the Heaven and the earth and all therein. I believe in God and His word. So, if God made the earth, then to me it is 'Sacred Ground.' I want to do my best to respect the land and waters and do not believe that God would want us to destroy or pollute His Creation. We are accountable for our actions that destroy any part of this earth.

Some people may not think it necessary to protect our environment and natural resources. Some may think that we should just get ready to go to heaven—never mind our land, water and air. Each of us should be prepared to meet the Good Lord, but I also believe that we should be good stewards of what He has blessed us with on this earth. In heaven, the streets will be paved with gold and I am sure the Lord would not want garbage littering those streets, just as I am sure He would not want it here either. It all belongs to Him. Shouldn't we begin the practice of cleaning up our highways, air and water? Perhaps then we will be less likely to slip up and throw something on those streets in heaven.

It must be the Indian blood within my veins that provokes me to question the destruction of our great country and everything within it. Why is it so hard to take care of something He gave us for only a short while? God owns this land and allows us to use it. One day, He will return and take it all away.

For a moment, can you imagine with me the dream that I have had about this great country? It goes something like this, "While traveling this beautiful country, I notice the land, rivers, lakes and streams and how pure and clean they are. It makes me thirst for a cool drink of water. I hear the birds singing with happiness, I see wild animals drinking from a clear, pure stream and even see fish swimming in the clearest of waters. The humans treat the earth and all that dwell within with the greatest of respect. Everyone is honest, compassionate and forgiving. People visit their neighbors and kinfolk and find joy in doing so. Most of all, everyone works in harmony for the good of all mankind. I look to the West and see one of the most beautiful sights I have ever seen—the sun is beginning to set. An artist could never capture the beauty or thrill of this view. I stand and watch until the sun has completely set and then, with a whisper I say, 'Thank You Lord'. As night comes, I look upward to the heavens and can see the moon and all the stars. After a while, I began to wonder if those stars are still in the same place they were when God created the universe. In the distance, I hear a hoot owl calling out and even further away I hear the bark of a hound dog. I feel peace in my heart as I stand listening to the sounds of the night. In the wonder of it all, a voice speaks to my heart saying, 'You know son, this is how it is supposed to be.' "

Maybe one day soon we will have a governor that will take a stand for Alabama. Maybe he will say, 'Alabama is not going to be a garbage dump any longer and this great state will be cleaned up and we will keep it that way.' Then as the tourists travel through our great state and read that sign that says, *Alabama the Beautiful*, they will think it is beautiful too!

Just maybe this will happen one day!

Coxey, Alabama 1930-1950

Coxey was the largest settlement between Athens and Rogersville, Alabama. If you purchased a ticket traveling west on the Trail Ways Bus Line from Athens to the Lauderdale County Line, then you bought a ticket to Coxey.

Coxey seemed to have it all as two of the largest, cleanest and best rivers in the state bordered it; on the south side is the Tennessee River and on the north side is the Elk River. Neither trash nor garbage was ever seen along the banks or floating down stream. The water was so clean that if you were thirsty, you could get a drink straight from the river and some of the best fish in the country was found in these two rivers.

Coxey was a great place to hunt because there were plenty of squirrels, rabbits, dove and quail which made for some mighty fine eating. One of my biggest thrills was hunting at night for opossum. Listening to the dogs tree the possum was the most peaceful sound in the world to me. On occasion when I got one Mom would bake it along with sweet potatoes. If you could overcome the greasiness of the possum it wasn't such a bad meal.

Located in the heart of Coxey was a Post Office and general store occupying the same building. Two of the world's nicest people, Mr. and Mrs. Jimmy Easter, operated them both. Mrs. Ida Easter resembled the woman on the label of *Mother's Cocoa*--she was beautiful.

When I was just a towhead, I decided that I needed to go to the store. Upon arrival I said to Mr. Easter, "I want to buy five dollars' worth of them big banana kisses." Suspiciously Mr. Easter asked, "Where did you get that five dollar bill?" I informed him that I had found it in the ditch down near my house. He said, "You need to go and tell your mom about this." Well, unfortunately for me, but fortunately for my mom, her brother Donald Howard happened to be inside the store too, so he took it upon himself to lead me back home. When we arrived he told Mom, "Sis, you'd better look and see if you are missing five dollars!" That day I learned a lesson called *Reasons You Never Want to Go to the Store and Attempt to Buy Five Dollars' Worth of kisses*! My mother applied that lesson with a hickory stick.

A short distance down the road and west of the Post Office was another general store operated by Mr. Ed Graham. Mr. Ed was an ole time fiddle player and his store was the gathering place if we wanted to play music. He had the only recording machine in Coxey during that time.

Traveling east from the Post Office on the hill was Clements High School. It was the smallest high school with the smallest gymnasium in the county, however, some of the best teachers and principals worked there.

After I made it through elementary school and my hooky playing days, I began to realize just what I had at Clements High School. Although the *Home of the Mighty Colts* had the smallest gym, it did not seem to make a difference to anyone. It was a unique school with a cozy place to play basketball and for a few years produced more winning teams than any other county school.

It was both an honor and privilege to have played for our great coach Warren Jenkins. The credit for our winning team must be given to him and I was fortunate enough to have played ball with some of the best players; William McElyea, Rex White, Edward Bridges, Benton Ball, Pete Draper, J. H. Bullington, Carol Sutton, William Ray Chittam, Bobby White, Jerry Sutton and Bobby Ray Flannagan. The cheerleaders were an important part of our team, too. It's only natural to play your best when you have good looking girls cheering you on so 'Thank You' to Bobbie Bradford, Marjorie Tribble, Amelia Sims and Vaughan Bridges. You were the greatest and Clements High was known to have some of the best looking girls in the county.

Just across the highway, there were two more general stores. Mr. Poke Allen operated the store on the south side of the highway and this particular store sat high off the ground so on the weekends the steps leading to the front porch served as a stage for Ray Taylor and Owen Gilliam who played country music. Ray always sang, *I'll just tell the world I've crossed you off my list* and I enjoyed listening to them.

Across the highway, Mr. Nick Bridges operated his store; however, it was the hangout for the tobacco chewing, snuff dipping, domino and checker playing, storytelling (including a few lies) men. One might say it was the *Head Quarters* for the latest Coxey news.

Just behind this establishment was a cotton gin owned my Mr. Tom Ezell. We spent many late hours there waiting to get a bail of cotton ginned off and if meal time came while we were there, we visited Mr. Nick's store to purchase a dimes worth of cheese and bologna—the crackers were free! Two nickels bought both a sixteen ounce Double Cola and a big Moon Pie, considered a hungry man's meal.

Up the highway about a half mile was the Log Cabin. It was also a general store, owned and operated by several different folks through the years.

Just past the Red Hill community was another general store operated by Mr. Fred Sims. The gas pump required both work and patience as one had to pump the gas into the glass bowl at the top of the pump, and then allow it to flow down into the gas tank. Mr. Fred had some very good looking daughters who on occasion worked in the store, what I called an added attraction.

6

A short distance past Mr. Fred's store was another one operated by Mr. Pat Shaw whom my dad, Alburn Casteel, always thought a lot of. Dad enjoyed visiting his store and talking with him and my brother Jimmy and I enjoyed tagging along.

Coxey had the only fort ever built in the United States to protect Native Americans from intruding white settlers. Fort Hampton was unique and I feel it should have been designated as a state park, however, since it was for the Indians, it was just forgotten.

My Uncle Jim and Aunt Flora Rose lived across the road from the Post Office. At one time he was a Limestone County Deputy Sheriff and on occasion, my dad made wine and home brew. Uncle Jim didn't want to know about this, but his son J. B. Rose sure did. He liked to slip off down to our barn for a taste every now and then.

As a young boy growing up in Coxey, I knew that I was one of the lucky ones. I loved this community, this country and the values which they were built on. Growing up at that time and in this area afforded me a good life. At a very early age, I learned to work in the fields and to respect my parents and our neighbors. Although we were probably considered poor folks, I never thought that way. I enjoyed life too much! How could a poor boy have that much fun?

I grew up in the best times this country has ever known, never bored a day in my life. There was never enough time to do all the things I wanted to do. Provide me with a fishing pole, a creek or riverbank and I was a happy boy. Give me a gun with some woods or fields and I was a happy boy. Give me a night with the moon and the stars shining, the sound the whippoorwill and owl, the old hound dog barking off in the distance and then I was an overjoyed boy!

The hardworking, honest and God fearing people who helped their neighbors in time of need made Coxey a great community. Most of the homes did not even have a lock on the doors.

My granddaddy, Abraham Bud Casteel, for a time was an operator on the Stewart Ferry, located behind Mt. Carmel Church of Christ. Some referred to him as Bud and some as Abe and he was the kindest and most gentle man I have ever known.

As I began to venture out into other parts of the country, I told people that I came from Coxey, Alabama. They would inform me that they had never heard of it so I asked if they ever heard of Coxey's Army. If their answer was 'Yes' then I informed them that this is where they came from.

By the way, Coxey did have an Army that served in the Korean War. They were attached to Company B of the 1343rd Combat Engineers. Among the group were three sets of brothers: Rupert and Richard McElyea, Buster and Happy Lovell and me and Jimmy Casteel. We served along with William McElyea, Harry Kerr, Babe Goode, Lynn Wright, Richard McMunn, Billy Legg, Bobby Davis, Harold Smith, William H. Shirley, Jerry Durham, Herbert Chittam and Robert L. Grigsby. One might have thought that the 'Athens Boys' were the brains of the unit, however, the 'Coxey Boys' were the heart and soul of it.

Some may ask what kind of activities the youth had available to them? Well, other than working, hunting, fishing and camping, we had some of the fiercest corncob battles the law allowed. Sunday afternoons it was like war at times. Some of the longest and drawn out Rook games, which usually extended into the night, were held at Lovell's home place, however, once the boys were old enough to like girls, they, me included, did a lot of walking and courting.

When I was in need of a good story, I walked to Gene McElyea's house, the best teller of tall tales of anyone I've ever known. He told them in such a way that you might actually think you were at the movies. I thought the world of that old man and sill miss him.

Another special person was Robert Chittam, alias Chittam Bob, or Bob Robert. I was fortunate to grow up in the same community with that very kind and gentle person who had a smile for everyone he met. He contributed to the fond memories of my hometown—Coxey, Alabama.

The Americans

The most mistreated people that ever lived on the American continent, and the only real Americans in the truest sense of the word, were the Native American Indians. They treated this country with the greatest respect and from what I have read, they were a very happy people with a way of life that endured for thousands of years.

It takes a great race with much honor and pride to exist in a country for many years without polluting the environment. It was as clean and unspoiled as it is was the day they arrived. Here is how I imagine the days of those early Native Americans:

"I see a race of people that were content with their lives because they had plenty of food, pure water and clothing to keep them warm during the winter months. They seem to have possessed a love in their hearts for their families and praise in their hearts to the Great Spirit that provided this Great Land for them.

"I see a healthy race that had little sickness and no worry for material possessions. They only took from the land what was needed to provide for their families.

"I see a race that was never exposed to the teachings of 'The Word of God', but probably lived closer to Him than any other race. It may be that God knew these people did things right anyway."

It brings a deep sadness to my heart when I think of the difficult times they experienced. Do we, as Americans, realize what our forefathers did to them?

The white man's standards were quite different from those of the Native American. It appears that they were looked upon as low class and ignorant with no rights to this great land upon which they had lived for so many years. Many white men felt compelled to run the Indians off the land or kill them if necessary.

The more the white man infiltrated the lands the more they were pushed off and away from their homes. Although more and more of the white men came, the Indians fought back but to no avail. Many of them and their entire families lost their lives in the fight for what once belonged to them. One day our government decided to step in and they did! Native Americans were rounded up like cattle and ordered off their land and onto reservations—possibly one of the biggest mistakes ever made by the United States Government.

Although both the white man and the Indian signed peace treaties, most of them were eventually broken by the white men.

As a human being, can you just imagine being corralled with your entire family and made to leave the place in which you were born, raised and lived? This was their home but they had no voice in what was about to happen. Can you imagine a march of many hundreds of miles with very little food and little or no clothing for the cold winter months? Can you imagine watching your baby, your mother or your father die from starvation? I wonder how the young and old continued to move along the path with frozen hands and feet. Those that could not make it eventually fell by the wayside and froze to death. Many also experienced various diseases contracted from the white man. The only element of truth about the entire march would be the name it was given, *The Trail of Tears.*

Often, I have thanked God for the blood in my veins that represents part of my heritage. My great grandmother, Annie Moore, was a full-blooded Native American who barely missed The Trail of Tears. My heart will forever bleed for her people and the pain they experienced on that march.

It is still a disgrace the way some Native Americans have to live. It seems as if no one really cares. We owe them more than we can ever repay. Has our government really tried to compensate them for the pain, sorrow and loss forced upon them?

As a young boy, I enjoyed watching cowboy and Indian movies. Sometimes I caught myself rooting for the Indians to win. When the kids played cowboys and Indians, I always wanted to be an Indian because I knew how to make a bow and arrow.

Some of my greatest heroes were Gene Autry, Roy Rogers, Daniel Boone, Davy Crockett, Sgt. York, Audie Murphy, John Wayne, the Lone Ranger and Tonto.

My Indian heroes were Sitting Bull, Crazy Horse, Red Cloud, Chief Joseph and Sequoyah but I guess Geronimo was my greatest Native American hero because he fought the longest and the hardest to save his family and their way of life. He agreed to surrender to the government with approximately thirty-five of his people left promised that he and his warriors would be allowed forty acres of land each if they would spend two years in prison in Florida. He died twenty-two years later still in prison—yet another promise broken by the white man.

Searching for Indian artifacts while walking along the fields and on creek and riverbanks is something I've always enjoyed. Whenever I found a good arrowhead, I would gaze at it for a long time as I imagined the person who had made it. Was he a great hunter? Did he have a wife and children or was he a younger person? How long ago was it made? What did their homes and campsites look like? Did they sit around the campfire at night and tell tall tales of long ago?

I tried to imagine the sounds they might have heard during that time and then realize that the only sounds they could have heard were the sounds of nature and their own voices.

If any of my ancestors participated in the round up of the Indians for the march that led them away from their homes and land, I pray that God will forgive them and the shame that was applied to the white man.

Although many years have passed, I wish to extend my apologies to all the great tribes of Native Americans throughout this country for the great wrongs and mistreatment afflicted upon their ancestors when the white man moved onto their land.

They were a people that loved this country, their family and their way of life and I respect and honor their ancestors for fighting to protect their families and way of life so dear to them.

Some have experienced a good life and some have even become movie stars, who by the way were much better at playing the part of an Indian than were the white men. However, the majority still live below the poverty level and many have given up hope of doing better.

Native Americans were one of the greatest races who have lived in America and I could never condemn them nor their way of life before the whites intruded. Was it wrong of them to hunt wild game for meat, grow a garden for vegetables, build their own homes, spend time with their families or experience the beauty of nature each day?

I believe I could give up the Rat Race we seem to be in today and might even be able to forsake all the modern technology and conveniences we have grown so accustomed to for that kind of lifestyle—a simpler way of life. But who am I to say that simple is better? I have always been a dreamer!

The Way It Was

Sometimes, I stand in awe thinking about all the problems we have in this country today and then I wonder, 'How could we have gotten in this situation in such a short period of history?

My mind wanders back to the times when I was growing up. We kids had to work in the fields to help make a living. Even if we were not working in the cotton fields, we had other chores to do such as cutting wood for the cook stove and heater. We stayed very active.

The food we ate came from our gardens. The fertilizer we used was chicken and cow manure. We did not spray poisons on our vegetable to keep insects off them; we used old remedies. The meat we ate was from chickens and hogs we raised. We fed the chickens corn we ground ourselves and fed the hogs corn and table scraps. We were supplied milk from our cow and eggs from our chickens.

The food we ate during the winter months was food Mom had canned from our garden. We also dried apples and peaches and she made jams and jellies from wild blackberries, plums, grapes and other fruits we gathered. She even canned fish and cooked it like salmon patties. We may have been considered poor folks but we ate well.

We were slim and trim. The good food we ate and the fact that it was unprocessed made the difference along with hard work.

We ate wild game we killed and fish we caught from our clean rivers. We didn't eat meat every day other than for breakfast from the hog meat in the smokehouse. Meat was usually reserved for a Sunday treat.

We were friends with all our neighbors and enjoyed visiting with them. I don't remember hearing of people dying from cancer or having heart attacks. As kids, we were hardly ever sick and if we did get sick our parents knew how to doctor us.

We lived in homes without air conditioning so fresh air came in through the open windows day and night all summer. Most homes had no locks on their doors or hooks on the screen doors. Violence, robbery and break-ins were not a worry for us during those years.

We were never in a hurry to go places and most of our travel was on foot or riding in wagons. Sometimes we caught the Trailways bus and went to Athens and when we did get to ride in a car, it was old and very slow.

Like other mothers, my mom put three meals on the table every day at about the same time. If we were at some of our friend's home during a meal time, we were always invited to eat with them. Most of the moms in the community were very good cooks.

People enjoyed the simple things in life back then. I remember my dad sitting outside under a shade tree on Sunday whittling the afternoon away while mom sat nearby. We kids counted the cars that passed by—on a good day there might be as many as five or six cars, including trucks.

The things we enjoyed in those days would be considered very dull to people today but what made life so good back then was that we had time to be happy. We knew that we had to obey our parents and that the principal and teachers were in charge at school. When one did something wrong and got caught, they knew what the punishment would be and I can testify to that. When you know what you can do and what you can't do, it makes life a lot simpler.

Bad storms were not a big threat to us. When it came up a bad looking cloud, we never thought about a tornado. We knew it was going to rain and maybe the wind would blow hard but we didn't fear that.

None of the kids back then ever thought of looking for something to make them high. We were high on life and there were no withdrawals from that kind of high.

Then one day progress showed up and things were never the same—not ever. Now we have all kinds of bad weather and deadly diseases. Just maybe the Creator is trying to tell us that we are not doing the right things or treating this earth with the respect it deserves. I believe the biggest disease to ever hit this country is greed.

The Elk River - My Childhood Playground

When I was a young boy growing up with my friends in our community next to the beautiful Elk River, it was the focal point where we congregated to enjoy life. We hunted, fished and camped out along it. Sometimes we borrowed a watermelon from someone's patch in the heat of the day and cooled it off in the river before eating it.

The Elk River was full of great tasting fish. We could sit in one place and catch all we needed for cooking. There wasn't much driftwood along the banks but if we found a piece or two we used them on our campfires. We never saw tin cans, bottles, plastic bags, old rubber tires or any other kind of garbage along the riverbanks. Life was truly joy in those days.

The water was so clean that if we got thirsty, we just got a drink from the river. That's what the birds and wild animals did and it never hurt them. Some of the best chicken stews I ever ate were made from the waters of Dement Creek. We lived the good life and heard the happiness in bird's songs and saw it in all the wild animals.

Nowadays if I walk along the banks of that same river, I become very sad and hurt because I am looking at one of the largest garbage dumps in North Alabama. How did this happen? In only sixty years it went from a beautiful, clean river to a polluted and poisoned body of water. It is now full of trash, debris and driftwood. The river is now filling in from all the garbage and top soil washing into it.

Sometimes I wonder if all the progress made in the past sixty years is worth the price we will pay down the road. We can't keep on doing what we are doing to this earth and our rivers, lakes and streams and still expect to have a place to live in the future.

As I recall my younger days, I realize that we have lost so much—the great chestnut trees once so plentiful along the river and throughout this country. The wild plum trees have nearly all died off. The blackberries, wild grapes and other berries are slowly vanishing. Many of the red oak trees are dying and the fish population is slowly dwindling away due to the polluted water.

We have lost so much in this country but our biggest loss is the respect for our Mother Earth—and that is a real shame because God gave us this to live upon and be happy. Somewhere along the way, the people have lost respect.

There is an old saying that I believe to be true: "What goes around, comes around." I believe that every harmful thing we do to

Mother Earth will come back to haunt us. We will pay someway or somehow down the road of life.

As I listen to the birds and wild animals nowadays, they don't have that happiness in their voices as they in yesteryears. It sounds more like a tear in their voices—maybe they are trying to tell us something.

The Elk River is still very special to me—not only because I grew up next to it and enjoyed it so much, but because my Native American ancestors lived next to it. It was their homeland and provided them with food and clean water. That is all they needed to be happy people until one day the U. S. Government decided they were not good enough to live on their own land, rounded them all up and drove them on *The Trail of Tears* march that took them far away from this river.

I believe time is running out for the people living on the earth today. If we don't soon wake up and try to turn things around and treat this earth like the Creator intended for us to do, our children's children just may not be able to survive on this poisoned and polluted country.

Listen to God Speaking

God speaks to His people in many ways.
If you don't think God has spoken to you
Just walk into the forest and
Listen to the wind gently blowing through the trees.

Listen to the sounds of all the wild animals.
Listen to the beautiful sounds of the birds singing.
Listen to the water gently flowing over the rocks in a small stream.

God made all of this
How can you not hear Him speaking to
You through all of these sounds?

The Last Trail for a Great Warrior

Walter Hill is someone I never took the time to meet and now I know a great opportunity was missed. I knew of him and where he lived but I did not know his character or anything else about him.

The Lord gives us many opportunities during our lifetimes, but we only take a advantage of a few of them and one regret I will always have is that I did not take the opportunity to meet him.

Walter Main Hill, of the Mohawk Tribe, was born July 23, 1925 at the Six Nations Reservation, Ontario, Canada and died June 14, 2003 in the Coxey community of Athens, Alabama. On June 23, 2003 a memorial service was held for him at his home place.

As I sat and listened to the words spoken about him, I realized just what a great man he was and how devoted he was to the Creator. This was a not a sad gathering for a man who had died but a celebration for a life and the way it had been lived. The more I heard about him from those who knew him best, the more I understood just what kind of person he was.

I saw . . .

Walter Hill was a person that loved the God who had created him and who gave God the honor, glory and praise for all things. He was a man who loved his family very much and also loved friends and neighbors, treating them with the greatest of respect.

He was a proud yet humble man; a strong man yet a possessor of a meek and caring heart; a wise man with much knowledge yet willing to listen to others express their views and beliefs. He was a man dedicated to helping others whether it was a spiritual or health problem or if they simply needed someone to tell their troubles to. Walter Hill was always available for anyone in need.

As a Mohawk medicine man, one of the greatest honors bestowed upon a Native American, he must have spent considerable time learning the ways and customs of his people and the herbs and their various uses.

16

Whenever I hear of a medicine man, a religious person with a vast knowledge of things, I am reminded of a scripture in the Bible that states "God put the herbs and plants on this earth to heal our bodies." I find it difficult to believe that anything artificial or synthetic is good for the body God created for us.

The words spoken by Les Tate, Ronnie Ray and Don Rankin at Mr. Hill's memorial service touched each and every heart in attendance. All the good things said about Walter Hill made me realize what an honor and privilege it would have been to have known and spent time with him.

At the service, I heard people say things like . . .

"When you look up and see a beautiful blue sky, how can you not believe that God made this?"

"When you look to the west at the most beautiful sunset, how can you not believe that God did this?"

"When you look around and see the mountains, rolling hills, trees, rivers, lakes and streams, how can you not believe that God created all this?"

"When God made this Great Earth and everything therein in only six short days, how can you not believe there is a God?"

If everyone could get their heart on the same level as Native Americans, who see this earth as Mother Earth, treat it with the greatest respect and realize that God created it for them for only a short while, then . . .

Maybe the greatest desires in our hearts would not be for money, wealth, riches and power.

Maybe we would enjoy our neighbors and even discover once again who our kinfolk are.

Maybe we would take a walk in the woods, listen to the bird sing, watch the animals play and rediscover what nature is all about.

Maybe we would find joy in spending time with our spouse or sweet heart in the country on a moonlit night away from the hustle and bustle of the city and listen to the sounds of the night and inhale the sweet fragrance of honeysuckle blooms.

Dreams of Lone Elk

Maybe we would be surprised by how much joy there still is in identifying the Big Dipper, the Little Dipper, the North Star and the Milky Way and yes, there are still stars in the sky.

It makes me proud that Walter Hill chose our community in which to live and call home after leaving the Six Nations Reservation. It makes me proud that our community had the only fort (Fort Hampton) ever built in the United States to protect the Indians from white intruders.

Walter is on his trail now which will carry him to and all across heaven—a trail that will last forevermore.

Just maybe my last trail will lead me to that same place. Maybe I will get to meet Walter after all and then we can sit around a campfire at that Great Pow Wow in heaven.

Walter left this to his friends:

Remember what I taught you . . .

When you pray, give thanks for what the Creator has given you. Ask for nothing because the Creator knows what you need more than you do yourself. If you receive a gift, give thanks to the Creator for putting the thought in the person's mind. Give thanks when you awake that you were able to draw another breath. Give thanks when you go to bed for having lived another day. Look around you and give thanks for what you see at that time. Think of the Creator all the time.

Walter Hill

Highway Seventy-Two—the Trail

All my younger life was spent living next to Highway Seventy-Two though I was born in the Blackburn community and later moved to the Coxey community. I grew up walking this highway when it was still a dirt and gravel road. There was always something very special about it to me but I didn't know what it was at the time.

Later in life I found out that Fort Hampton was located just a little way behind our home in Coxey. It was built to protect Native Americans from the white settlers moving into the area and still later I

18

learned that my great grandmother was a full-blooded Native American Indian.

It was sometime later that I learned that Highway Seventy-Two was a very old road and that the first people to travel it when it was still just a trail were the Native American Indians.

In the eighteen thirty's the Indians in this part of the country were rounded up and forced to leave their homes and lands to march on the trail taking them to the Oklahoma Territory. That trail later became well known as the *Trail of Tears* but is now known simply as Highway 72.

Many Indians died on this cruel forced march. Many died from white man's sicknesses, many were killed by soldiers and many froze to death. They were buried along the trail as they continued westward. All Indians regard their burial grounds as holy or sacred places and it is forbidden for anyone to disturb them, though that didn't matter to most white people.

As I look at Highway 72 now, all I see is a garbage dump. I've never seen a road anywhere with so much trash and junk on the sides of the road. I find it hard to believe that the State of Alabama or Limestone County has allowed this to happen—I thought we had litter laws, but I guess not.

This highway needs to be cleaned up. It should be renamed the *Trail of Tears Highway.* It needs to have a monument erected at a special place along it paying tribute to those Native Americans who perished and were buried along the *Trail of Tears.*

This highway should be treated with the greatest respect and honor because it is a burial ground for many Native Americans.

Many say that this is a deadly highway because of the numbers who have been killed in car wrecks along it and it needs a lot of construction done to it. It needs to be completely redone but I also know that when you disturb an Indian burial ground that bad things will happen. They always do.

The state can make it the best highway in the state, but until we learn to respect and honor those buried along the trail by keeping it neat and clean, there will always be many deaths on this highway even if the state declares it the safest road in the country.

The Grand Ole Opry - *When the Opry Was Grand*

When I grew up we kids had to work very hard in the fields all week long trying to earn enough money to buy our school clothes and books. Sometimes on Saturday morning I caught the Trailways bus and went to Athens to see a great western movie. Athens had two movie theaters, the Ritz and the Plaza back then, and both showed western movies on Saturdays.

My heroes on the big silver screen were Gene Autry, Roy Rogers, Tex Ritter, Red Ryder and Little Beaver to name a few. After watching two movies, eating a hamburger and drinking a big Double Cola, I caught the bus back home to Coxey and imagined myself being a cowboy like Gene, Roy or Tex. They were the good guys, the ones I looked up to.

Saturday nights became very special to me after dad bought our first radio because that's when the Grand Ole Opry was broadcast from Nashville on WSM. Sometimes our front porch was filled with people listening to the Opry and I saw the joy in our neighbor's faces as they smiled and kept time with the music by patting their feet.

There were singers like Eddie Arnold, Roy Acuff, Bill Monroe, Ernest Tubb, Kitty Wells, Grandpa Jones, Stringbean, Uncle Dave Macon and his son Doris, the Fruit Jar Drinkers, Rod Brasfield and Minnie Pearl, the Duke of Paducah, Jamup and Honey, and the boys from Alabama, Hank Williams, the Delmore Brothers, Lou Childers, Freddie Hart and the list goes on.

My Uncle, Henry Casteel, one of the best men I ever knew, owned and operated a school bus. Some Saturdays he took a load of people to Nashville to see the Grand Ole Opry. I tried to make all these trips and that is when I became exposed to live performances. What a joy it was to sit in the old Ryman Auditorium on a hot summer night with everyone cooling themselves with their church fans. As long as I could watch and hear my favorite country singers, I didn't care how hot it was or how much I sweated.

From an early age I knew that I wanted to be a country music singer. My brother Jimmy and I had a shared bicycle and he had an old

Stella guitar so I traded my half of the bicycle for the old guitar. I went to work trying to play and stuck with it until I learned a few chords. Next I tried to sing and strum.

Now I had a dream and goal to someday be on stage at the Grand Ole Opry singing my heart out. I wasn't a good singer but believed that if I worked hard enough my dream just might come true so I listened to country music every chance I could and strummed by old guitar and sang.

About this time other singers were becoming members of the Opry; singers like George Morgan, George Jones, Carl Smith, Billy Walker, Loretta Lynn and three beautiful women I fell in love with; Dolly Parton, Connie Smith and Dottie West. That love has never faded. Some more Alabama greats were Sonny James, Vern Gosdin and Ernie Ashworth.

Country music was at its best during that time and I don't believe it will ever be that good again. Back then the singers sang from the heart and their songs told stories about love and hurting and good times. They loved what they did but nowadays it's become a money thing and all the bands and singers sound too similar.

The greatest part in any dream or goal is the working for it and wanting your dream to come true. After achieving your goal the joy sort of fades away so you might say I am one of the happiest country music singers that never made it because I still experience the joy that comes from wanting it to happen.

It's just not the same so I don't listen to the Grand Ole Opry much anymore. It's hard to convert an old country music fan to the new country music style though I still enjoy listening to the radio stations that still play the classic country music and it still sounds as good today as it did so long ago.

Sometimes in my mind, I still picture myself sitting in the Ryman listening to Hank Williams, Eddie Arnold, Ernest Tubb and the other greats who once graced the stage of the Grand Ole Opry.

My Purpose

Everyone is put on this earth for a purpose I believe. Some don't find it until later in life. Because God put it in my heart to help the Native American Indians, it sometimes makes my heart very sad and grieved because it seems like a hopeless task since most people have forgotten them, but I made a vow to my God that I would work for the rest of life to help them.

We go to church on Sunday morning wearing our fine clothes and driving our fine automobiles and sit there and listen to the preacher talk about what we need to do to go to heaven. We have been blessed in Limestone County with some very good and dedicated preachers and some good churches, but I have never heard one preacher say anything about making amends to the Indian people for what our white ancestors did to them.

Sitting there, I wonder if we are worthy of calling ourselves Christians while true Americans are deprived of so much while living on reservations, starving to death where unemployment is as high as eighty percent.

It seems that churches want to send their people on foreign missions to help those people and that is a good thing, but how can we not see how the Indian people have to live and not want to help them? The irony of it all is that most of them are probably our distant relatives.

God has a people that are very special to Him because they did things right while living on this earth. They took care of what He created and they looked to Him for all their needs. Oh how He must have loved those who never had the love of money in their hearts.

The Indian schools out west have my gratitude for requesting a copy of my book, *The End of the Trail of Tears* to put in their libraries. I also want to thank the schools of Cullman, Jefferson and Walker Counties for using this book in their history classes. Also special thanks go to Gardendale, Alabama and the state of Tennessee where it is doing so well.

God gave me a purpose in life and I am grateful to Him for that. I am grateful it was to help the Native American Indians because they are a very special people to me. I will do my very best at this assignment.

22

Every story I have written was inspired by my God. There is no way I could write a story without Him.

It would be an eye opening experience if churches sent their young people on a mission trip to the Indian reservations out west and let them see how true Americans are forced to live. Let them see the shacks; let them see a once proud and noble race that has been beaten down to nothing by our white ancestors. They would see that not everything is right in America. Maybe they would be touched enough to see that things could be better for them if we did a little more of what God would like for us to do—and that is to just lend a hand.

The Ladies I've been in Love With - *(That Never Knew Me)*

When very young, I loved to go to Athens on Saturday mornings to see the great western movies. Growing a little older I had the opportunity to go to the movies during the week, too.

There was one movie I remember seeing called *The Dolly Sisters,* starring Betty Grable and June Haver. Well, I simply fell head over heels in love with those two women and thought, "How could God make anyone so beautiful?" I had never seen girls who looked that that before.

Growing older became my desire so I could marry one of them. Many days were spent in the cotton fields thinking about them. Maybe that's the reason I didn't mind working hard because Betty and June were on my mind. I stayed in love with them for a long time and deep down inside I guess I still am.

The next lady to capture my heart was very beautiful, tall and slender with long, red hair. Rita Hayworth was her name and *Gilda* is the movie I most remember her starring in. Like the first two, I flipped for her and then wondered which of the three I would choose to settle down with.

After some time another beautiful lady showed up on the screen and I saw right then that God had outdone Himself. She had beautiful blond hair and the rest of her was gorgeous too. Marilyn Monroe really caught my eye and sort of made me forget about the other three so I knew right off she was the one for me.

Every movie she was in just made me fall deeper in love with her. You might say she was the love of my life but I noticed that she was not always a happy person which made my heart sad for her but that just made me lover her more.

There were many who said bad things about her but in my eyes I only saw the good. When she died, or I believe was murdered, I felt a deep loss. I will remember her for the remainder of my days.

Always a big fan of the Grand Ole Opry stars, there were three beauties I fell in love with there too; Dolly Parton, Dottie West and Connie Smith.

Dolly had the biggest, most beautiful smile, one of the reasons I loved her so much and Dottie was a beauty with her long, auburn hair. I shed some tears when she died in a car wreck.

Before I ever saw her, I fell in love with Connie's voice. What a joy it was to see how beautiful she really was. She is everything one could ever want in a female country music star; the voice, the looks and the personality. No one touched my heart with a song like Connie and I will always be in love with her.

When I was younger, I tended to fall in love with older women, but now that I'm older, I seem to fall in love with younger ones. The lady who has my heart now may be the last one I fall in love with—who never knew me. She is a great actress, beautiful, has a beautiful smile and seems to be kind and gentle. Her movies are always great and it was easy to fall in love with Sandra Bullock. Sandra, you will always be in my heart.

Some folks may consider this story a bit on the foolish side but they would have to admit that my taste in women ain't bad.

Hog Killing Time - *(Has its Ups and Downs)*

During my early years folks got excited when hog killing time rolled around because we knew our bellies would be filled with good,

24

fresh hog meat. It always happened about the same time each fall because it remained cold all winter and the meat wouldn't spoil.

In our family, Uncle Jim Rose was always in charge of the hog killing and he did the shooting of the hogs, but one year he told my brother Jimmy and me, "I am going to let you two do the killing. One of you will do the shooting and the other one will stick the hog in the throat with a knife so he will bleed out."

Jimmy was the elder so he spoke up and said, "I will do the shooting and you can cut his throat." I had no problem with that because it seemed that cutting a hog's throat while lying lifeless on the ground would be no trouble. Uncle Jim told Jimmy to use his rifle because he thought his was the best single shot rifle in Coxey. He told me to sit upon the rail fence and after Jimmy shoots, you jump off and cut the hog's throat.

Jimmy and I sat on the rail fence. Jimmy took aim and I was waiting to jump. The gun went off and I hit the ground jumping right on the back of that three hundred pound hog but he didn't fall to the ground. He carried me all over that hog pen. Sometimes I was on top of the hog and other times he was on top on me but finally, I got the chance to cut his throat.

After he stopped moving, I laid there beside the hog. Everyone waited for me to get up so they could tell which one was me and which was the hog.

Uncle Jim asked Jimmy, "Where did you shoot the hog?" Jimmy's reply was, "Right between the eyes." Uncle Jim crawled over the fence to inspect the hog. He looked the hog over then looked back at Jimmy, still sitting on the fence and said, "Boy, you shot the hog through the ear!"

J. B. Rose, my dad and everyone else laughed their insides out. Aunt Flora Rose came running down from the house to see what all the fun was about. It seemed to be her heart's desire to see me get into trouble so she had something to laugh at.

Still standing in the hog pen, covered with mud and blood from head to foot, I knew mom would not let me go into the house. The thought came to me to go to the creek to wash off but it sure was cold to do that.

Mom made me strip off all my clothes outside in the cold, and then she poured buckets of water over me to wash off the mud and blood. Of course, everyone was still watching and laughing their butts off.

A Friend and Storyteller

A good storyteller who can hold your attention with anticipation is something that most everyone has experienced in their lives. I believe I was blessed with one of the best.

He was a poor man who never had much, like most of us in the Coxey community, but he was a happy person who loved life and experienced the joy of it more than most people.

Gene McElyea was a very close and dear friend from my early days. His son William was one of my best friends. We went to school together, played baseball and basketball on the same team at Clements High School and lived within walking distance of each other.

All of us boys grew up in our community during a time when hunting, fishing and camping out on the creeks and riverbank was about the only thing to do if we were not in school or working on the farms. Work began at an early age back then.

We learned our hunting and fishing skills early. When we camped out at night we needed to learn how to cook for ourselves. Gene taught us many things about all these things. We spent all our spare time in the woods or on the riverbanks and they were the greatest joys in life while growing up.

Gene lived about a mile behind our house so when we began possum hunting at night, I walked through the fields next to Wallace Cemetery and on to their house. He always had pretty good hunting dogs. Mr. Louie Brooks lived just over the hill from Gene and he had a good hunting dog named Jack who always showed up to go hunting with us. Gene, William, Richard McElyea and I were the hunting crew most of the time but sometimes William's brother Frank B. and my brother Jimmy went with us.

The old house that Gene and his family lived in had a fireplace for heat, where we all gathered around to listen to him tell those tall tales about his hunting days as a youngster. He had the ability to make us feel as if we were right there with him.

Gene went with us many times on hunting trips and always wore overalls, a denim jacket he called his jumper and carried his walking staff along with a can of snuff in his pocket. It was a joy to have him along and listen to his stories but if for some reason he didn't go with us that would be the night he told us one of his scary stories before we left the house but that didn't deter us from going.

During some of our hunts the rain drizzled. That was a good night for hunting because the dogs could smell the possums better on wet ground. After about half the night we usually had three or four possums in the sack and Gene would say, "Boys, it's time to go on home now." By then we were wet and cold so we were ready to go. It felt so good to get home, get out of my wet clothes and crawl into a good, warm featherbed while listening to the rain on the tin roof until I fell asleep.

At one time, Gene had a dog named Jabbo he had traded for in Scottsboro on Trade Day. He was so old and slow that when he struck the trail, we had to wait about half an hour before he could tree a possum. If we caught as many as two possums with Jabbo in one night, he was worn out, so we took him back to the house.

As spring began our thoughts turned from hunting to fishing. Gene had many stories about is younger fishing days. One was about a huge catfish known as Ole Dennis that swam in the waters of the Elk River that had been hooked many times but no one had ever landed him. Every time Gene took us fishing he said, "Come on boys. Let's go catch ole Dennis!"

As far as I know Gene never had nor drove a car. He walked about everywhere he went and was never in a hurry to get there. If he saw something on the side of the road and didn't know what it was, he took his walking stick and moved it around until he figured out what it was. He then said a few choice words and moved on.

Even in our high school days, we continued hunting and fishing with Gene. By then he had several grandkids and some of them went with us. I like all of Gene's grandkids but James was special to me. We were buddies back then and he is still one of my best and dearest friends.

Gene never attended any of our ball games but he always wanted to know how we did and if we had won. William, Richard and I were in the National Guard and were called to active duty and sent to Korea.

Following the war, William continued to serve in the military. I chose to come home with an honorable discharge. My friendship with Gene and his family continued and we still had many happy days hunting in the woods and fishing on the river. Gene always treated me like his son though I'm sure he missed William very much.

A humble man, Gene never spoke an unkind word to anyone that I know of. He always had time for us boys and seemed to enjoy being with us. I never knew of him working a public job but he mostly farmed and always had money in his pocket. Because of his hawk bill nose and dark complexion, I believe Gene had American Indian blood in him; He looked to me like he might have been Choctaw.

The times I spent with Gene McElyea and his family contributed greatly to the joy and happiness I experienced in my life and I will always treasure those times. Looking back I realize that I walked many miles with that old man and loved every step of the way.

A People Still Hurting

The first mistake white men made after landing on the shores of this country was failing to become friends with the Native Americans. They could have learned so much from the Indians, especially about how to treat Mother Earth.

The whites were taken into the villages of the Native Americans because they were sick and nearly starved to death where they were fed, clothed and nursed back to health. Without their help, the white men would not have survived but sadly, once they regained their health, they had no respect for the Indians who saved them. They wanted nothing to do with them and felt the Indians were lower than animals and this is proven throughout history.

When they first arrived on Turtle Island, now renamed America, they had only one thing on their minds and that was to find gold! They knew they would be able to find it here in this lush, rich new land they claimed to have 'discovered'. In actuality the Native Americans had lived here for thousands of years before the pale-faced men ever set foot on it. They came to find wealth and riches here and were not going to let any innocent Indians stand in their way. The killing and murdering of Indians began because of their greed for gold and treasures.

Before their arrival, Indians had neither sickness nor disease among them. The country was clean and pure, the streams and rivers were so pure they drank from them without worry of becoming ill. That was the way the Creator had intended for it to be and life was joyous, filled with happiness and contentment.

As increasing numbers of 'settlers' came, they took away the Indians' land. All of Turtle Island belonged to them until that time but the intruders were never satisfied with only some land; they kept taking more and more and murdered them to do so. The Indians fought back but to no avail. Their weapons did not compare to the gunpowder of the white men so tens of thousands of innocent men, women and children were slaughtered until their population declined.

All the peace treaties made between Indians and the white government was broken by the white men. Then they found the most desolate and destitute lands in the country to create reservations where the remaining Native Americans were forced to live.

This all took place in the early 1800's but tragically they are still living on these dreaded reservations today. Each year many starve and freeze to death for lack of adequate food and shelter. This is America where people are supposed to be free and help each other, a Christian nation where needs are met and programs are set up to feed the hungry, warm the cold and shelter the homeless. But somehow it is failing for the Indians.

Something is wrong when people call this a Christian nation while the true, indigenous Americans must still live on these horrible, dirt poor reservations. Often, I have wondered how very sad our Creator must feel about them and how they are still being mistreated, even today.

Life is good for those in America who have new automobiles and plenty to eat yet the Indians on the reservations are given rations, if anything at all, yet many go to bed hungry each night. They sleep in the cold because they do not have heat in their homes and frankly, who really cares? How many people have taken time to find out about them, right in our own backyard? Yes, this is America; we are not talking about a third world country rather the good old United States of America. I care very deeply and I know the Creator cares too. The Bible says, "Vengeance is mine, sayeth the Lord". With all the hurricanes, tornadoes and other devastations today maybe His judgment has already begun for the way they have been mistreated.

If you are living a pretty good life today, try to imagine living the life of an Indian on a reservation. Picture living on a dirt road where dust covers your clothes, your skin and gets into your nose and eyes as you walk down the road to your house. Visualize going hungry night after night without light at the end of the tunnel, hopeless that anything will ever change for you. Create in your mind's eye attempting to stay warm in temperatures forty below zero when you only have a tiny heater, making you more blessed than many others. You may get the inside temperature of your home up to forty degrees but still have no hope of anything getting better. Try to imagine watching a newborn baby cry every night from hunger and sickness because its mother doesn't have enough milk due to malnutrition. No baby food is supplied to these families. They don't have money for a doctor and even if they did, they lack transportation to get to one. Folks, let me tell you, this happens every day on reservations.

We rob Mother Earth of her natural resources as fast as possible and all because of greed and wealth. Our precious earth has become so polluted and contaminated with chemicals that it is now dangerous for our health. Rivers, lakes, streams and highways look like garbage dumps and it was not Indians who did this. They respect the earth with great reverence as well as all wildlife. Now white people are dying off with all varieties of sickness and disease as a result of the pollution. The foods we eat, the water we drink and the air we breathe all have some type of chemicals or contaminates in them. The Indians' bond within their families is so strong that when an elder becomes old and sick, their number one priority is to care for them until they pass on.

As I am Cherokee, I grieve for these people. It doesn't matter what tribe they are. If you have compassion and want to help them, please feel free to contact me.

Living My Dream

As a very young boy I enjoyed being out in the woods and on the riverbanks. You might say I enjoyed living in the wild and wanted to live like the Indians did long ago. They are a great race and very special to me. During the summer I didn't want to wear a shirt so I could get a dark tan and wanted to let my hair grow long, but my parents wouldn't let that happen.

As I grew older I learned that my great grandmother was a full-blooded Indian. All ears, I wanted to find out everything I could about her. My grandmother told me that her mother was beautiful and one great lady, very humble and kind.

Tonto from *The Lone Ranger* radio program was my first Native American hero; I still have a picture of him sitting on his horse, Scout. From the time I first joined *The Lone Ranger Club* as a kid I have had many Indian heroes and always having felt they were my people, I collected items relating to them.

Growing into manhood, I still had Indian things in my home. Everyone knew how I felt about them and the Indians. My first two wives died from cancer and each of them was one of the best women God ever put on this earth. They accepted and shared the feelings I had for the Indians.

Following the death of my second wife, lost and lonely, and wondering what my purpose in life was after so much loss, voices began telling me to write about the events of my life so that is what I have attempted to do.

One rainy night in October 2003, I lay on my bed listening to the rain falling on the tin-topped roof as things I had heard about my great grandmother ran through my mind. Half asleep, a story unfolded in my mind. It was so real that I felt as if I was really there and later, voices told me to write the story. I believe it was my god and the spirits of my ancestors telling me this, so I wrote the book, *The End of the Trail of Tears*.

Early in 2005 it came from the printer so now I am living my dream. Along with J. B. Salter, who illustrated the book, I attend Indian festivals and Pow-Wows to sign my books. We have met some of the greatest people I have ever known; some full-blooded Indians and some are only part but all are Indians in my heart.

The book has sold well everywhere but Limestone County where I grew up. It has gone to three foreign countries and five Indian schools out west have requested copies for their libraries. Continually I receive phone calls from people thanking me for writing it.

In Lawrenceburg, Tennessee, the Cherokee Indian/David Crockett Museum has been a big promoter of my book, thanks to principal Chief Joe Sitting Owl White. With great respect I thank him for his help and I have been offered the position of Chief Clan Chief of the tribe. What an honor it is to live the dream I've had all my life.

Indians are people who are very close to the Creator giving praise and thanks to Him for everything in their lives. If there is a more religious group of people in this country, I have yet to meet them. They honor and pay tribute to the American soldiers more than any I know of and it is an honor for me to be living my dream with people so close to God.

Jesus Was in the Building

Mr. E. F. Bullington was principal of Clements High School during the 1940's and every morning before classes, the entire student body met in the auditorium for daily devotion. Mr. Bullington led the meeting and was known to ask different students to share a quote from the *Bible.* Hiding from his eagle eyes was not an option so you'd better have a quote ready to offer. This was when you knew Jesus was in the building.

Times were good back then. We knew the principal and teachers were in charge and what they said was law and most students looked up to them with great respect. Most of the students were friends and if there was ever a fight between any of them, they knew that afterwards there would be a price to pay—like a trip to the principal's office where the three-hole paddle hung on the wall.

As a member of the basketball and baseball teams, our coach, Mr. Warren Jenkins, always made sure we had a prayer before going onto the court or the field.

Mt. Carmel Church of Christ was across the road from the high school and during the summer months, they held their 'big meeting' just about the same time Uncle Jim Rose's watermelons ripened. The church was the old, white wooden building with tall windows along each side and the windows were opened all the way during the summer.

Many people walked to church; a few came in cars and some came in wagons pulled by mules or horses. Some of the boys sat outside on the wagon and listened to the service. Some of the best old time church singers I ever heard were in that congregation. They raised the rafters when they sang.

The song leader was Mr. Hous Smith; then there was Nell and Clarence Smith, Belle Lovell, Uncle Jim and Aunt Flora Rose, the McElyeas, Ezells, Bridges, Jenkins and many others. Mr. Hous pecked his tuning fork on the post in the middle of the church, sang his do-re-mis and everyone sang. You knew Jesus was in the building.

Sometimes we boys didn't go to the 'big meeting'. Instead we went over to Gene McElyea's house and sat on the front porch to listen to them sing. Gene always enjoyed us being there and even though the church was almost a mile away, we could pick out different ones voices—especially Nell Smith's. She could do some singing. Gene always had good words about those singers at Mr. Carmel Church.

Growing up in the Coxey community, we boys were very blessed, learning to hunt and fish at an early age. Some of our favorite things to do included camping out on the creeks and riverbanks where we swam a lot, cooked our food and I must say it was good. We spent many nights in the woods hunting for opossum. Because Jesus watched over us, we made it through those times without getting snake bit or drowned.

Four of us were in the same class at school and joined the National Guard when we were only about sixteen. We had tired of trying to court girls with only our cotton picking earnings so we figured that with the extra funds from the Guard, we might be able to buy our girlfriends hamburgers some of the time.

In August of 1950, as we prepared to begin our senior year we received orders that our unit had been mobilized into active duty. Now we were genuine members of the military. Following basic training, we left the United States and about thirty days later arrived in Pusan, Korea.

We awaited the arrival of our equipment for a few weeks in Pusan, and then headed north traveling through Inchon and Seoul. Those cities had just been bombed to the ground. We continued northward until we heard the big guns firing. As we passed the artillery, we knew our destination and asked Jesus to be with us.

Jesus was with us during those difficult months in Korea—long hard days and lonely nights with continuous gunfire, bitter cold winters and sweltering summers. We endured many scary times and experiences. Thanksgiving Day 1951 (war doesn't stop for holidays) we were in the Punch Bowl as snow mixed with freezing rain fell into our plates of our hot Thanksgiving meal making it cold and watery before we could eat it. That was a very lonely time but I could feel the presence of Jesus.

Many changes had taken place by the time we arrived home in 1952. People bought television sets for their homes, more folks were buying and driving new cars, toilets were moved inside the houses and progress was happening. People were definitely becoming smarter as new items were invented and developed so fast it made one's head swim.

No doubt about it, it was becoming a high tech world. People were so busy they no longer had time to be friends with their neighbors—then later came the computers, video games and cell phones.

People became so smart they kicked Jesus out of the schools and told the kids they could no longer talk to Him. Praying wasn't even allowed ball games and the government said, "It's the law. Take down those signs that display the Ten Commandments. We don't go by those rules anymore."

In the last seventy years, many changes have been made. Now I live in a different world than the one I grew up in. A simple, ordinary person finds it hard to understand all the things that happened and the changes that have been made. One good thing that has not changed is Jesus—He always stays the same.

The old Clements School was torn down many years ago but I still remember the laughter and happiness that rang throughout those old hallways and playground. The wooden building at Mt. Carmel Church also fell by the wayside along with the huge, beautiful trees in the churchyard where many dinners on the ground had been held, they had also served as hitching posts for the mules and horses. The wagon tracks have all been covered with concrete. Those trees were home to many July Flies and Dry Flies as they sang in harmony with the singers inside. Those old time singers are now singing for Jesus and if you listen closely you can almost hear Nell Smith above the rest.

Currently we have so many problems—drugs in the schools, sky high prices for everything, government officials getting caught for wrongdoings and greed is like a disease in this country. The old saying, "The rich get richer and the poor get poorer" holds true today more than ever.

Sometimes I wonder if the Lord is angry with people for the way they rob the natural resources of His creation. When God created this earth, it was made to support life forever. People are supposed to live in harmony with Mother Nature, taking only enough from the earth to supply their needs for life to exist.

Maybe if we work really hard to try and make a difference by doing things that are right and getting on our knees more often, things might just work out for the betterment of our world. I only hope and pray that Jesus doesn't give up on us and leave the building.

Rogersville – A Town I Remember

When very young, my family moved about two miles east of Rogersville across from Aunt Litha and Uncle Lee Cunningham. We lived there for only a short time and before moving back across the river into Limestone County.

It was then that my fondest memories of Rogersville began. We visited Aunt Litha and Uncle Lee's home often and frequently he loaded us cousins (Cunninghams, Grahams, Casteels, Souths and Roses) into the back of his old pickup truck and drove us into Rogersville and we sang the fight songs for each branch of the military as we rode to town. Sometimes he took us to the carnival so we could enjoy the rides.

One time we all went to a tent show set up just behind where Barclay Auto Parts is now located. It seems it was Jimmy Ogles tent show and it was a play with live actors performing which I had never before seen. During the play one actor pulled out a gun and shot another actor. Thinking the man was dead, I nearly jumped out of my skin. Unbeknownst to me at the time, they used blanks shells.

Along with Mr. Preston Guthrie, my dad Alburn Casteel worked in a barbershop located next to the south corner of what now is Lee Street and Highway 207. Sometimes my brother Jimmy and I went with dad on Saturdays to spend the day with him; it was fun to spend the day doing what boys do at the shop.

My first trip to the dentist was in Rogersville. The office was upstairs in a building just east of where East Lauderdale News is now located. More than anything else I remember the drill he used to grind my tooth and the foot pedal similar to the old sewing machines to operate it.

Just up the street going west was Plotts Drug Store. Choosing an old fashioned root beer, I tasted my first fountain drink there.

Sunny Bedingfield was a boy I met there; we became fast friends often meeting in town and hanging out together. He showed me the culvert that ran from where Spry's old building, which is still standing today and ended to the south side of what is now Lee Street. We were able to stand up and actually walk through that culvert. At the south end of the drain there used to be a service station.

Dad took me to Rogersville to buy my first pair of tennis shoes when I started playing basketball in high school. The store, operated by Mr. Poke Comer and Mr. Jomey Wilbanks, was where the music place is today on the north corner of Lee St. and Highway 207. It was like a general store displaying shoes, clothes and many other items. Later those two great men built and operated a grocery store across the street. The property is now home to an auto parts building.

There used to be an old house on the land where Barnett's Drug Store is now located with a huge mulberry tree in the front yard of the home and we played on the enormous roots of that awesome tree. It was very close to Lee Street which was once Highway 72, something a lot of people today do not realize.

While still young, a few other boys and I walked from Limestone County to Rogersville on Saturday afternoons to watch the picture show later that night. It took almost two hours to walk the distance to the theatre which was in an old building near the City Hall today. The building looked like an old western storefront and if memory serves me correctly Mr. Martin operated it. He hung two loud speakers on the front of the building and started playing music about an hour before show time. We were able to hear it as we came to the cemetery on the edge of town and it could be heard all over town.

One of the movies I remember best was *The Five Sullivan's,* a story revolving around five brothers on the same ship during World War II. The ship was bombed and all five were killed during the attack. The family had only one child, a daughter, left. Military regulations regarding brothers serving together in the same unit during wartime resulted as the story was based on fact.

Sometimes there was live entertainment in that old building. My favorite group was Autry Inman and his band.

From time to time, a carnival came to Rogersville so in addition to walking to the movies, we walked to the carnivals too. It was always set up where Hardees and the Foodland parking lot are today. When we topped the hill at Oliver we could see the Ferris wheel which piqued our excitement and increased our walking speed. On the long walk back home, we often laid down on the highway to rest, not worrying about cars as there were very few on the road in those days.

Rogersville was a booming little town back then. Along with the movie theater there was a restaurant that stayed open until midnight. After the movie we could stop by and get a hamburger and cold drink if we had enough money. It was located two or three doors behind the music place is today. Mr. Hannah, who operated it, had two beautiful daughters who worked there which was certainly an added attraction.

It was sometime later when someone built a new movie theater and it was a considerable improvement. Located near where the old Post Office used to be I saw my most memorable movie there *The Outlaw,* starring Jane Russell and Jack Buetel.

Barnett's old drugstore was near the restaurant but now most of those old buildings are vacant and deteriorating.

Rogersville had two taxi services then. Mr. Ferris Cooper owned and operated one and Mr. Tom Lentz owned the other. Both appeared to be very successful and they seemed to make a good living providing those services.

There were two doctors in town back then, Dr. Waddell and Dr. Rousseau. Both were well liked and thought of for being good and yes, they made house calls, even as far out as Limestone County.

The town had one police officer but don't remember his name. The probable reason is that he was not seen much because there was no crime that I'm aware of. The only occurrence I recall is when a man came into Hannah's Restaurant one night spouting off to another man who took it as long as he could stand before taking him outside by the nape of his neck and whipped the tar out of him!

Sometime after starting to play basketball, Rogersville came to Clements to play us one Friday night. If we didn't win it, it was a close game. The opposing team was disgusted for having to play in our small gym; the smallest in the area and even the ceiling was low. With every attempt at a long shot they hit the ceiling. A few weeks later we played them again in their gymnasium. The size of it intimidated us and when the game was underway we knew we were in trouble. They showed us no mercy and ran us to death on that long court. Harlan Hill, O'Neal Emery, John Robinson, Arlee Snoddy and more on their team were great players.

Rogersville was always a fun place for me and I will always be proud of that little town for supplying me with a heart full of good times and fond memories.

We Wonder What We Are Doing Wrong

A constant prayer and dream of mine for many years is that someday America would wake up and see just what they are doing to this country. So much destruction and many harmful things are being done to Mother Earth and anyone with common sense can see that we are destroying everything sacred about this planet.

God created all things and this earth was a beautiful sight to behold for a long time. Everything was clean and pure; there were magnificent mountains, beautiful lakes, rivers and streams, mighty oceans, rolling hills, plains and prairies with lovely trees, plants and flowers. It was so beautiful that I believe even God Himself was amazed at His work.

He made man superior to all other creatures on the earth and entrusted man to take care and watch over it because He made the earth for us to live upon and enjoy. The first occupants, the Native American Indians, did exactly that. They lived here for thousands of years, keeping it as clean and pure as when God made it and they lived free from many of the diseases we experience today.

Then one day the white race stormed into the country with wealth, riches and gold on their minds and in their hearts. In just a few hundred years we have robbed the earth of most the natural resources, polluted the rivers, lakes and streams while the air has become unfit to breathe. Our roadways, highways and waterways have turned into garbage dumps and *we wonder what we are doing wrong?*

Riding the highways and roadways in Alabama is no longer pleasant because of all the trash and junk along the roadsides. Why are our litter laws not enforced? Visitors travelling through the state will pass judgment on what type of people we are once they see our roadsides.

And exactly what have we received from the pollution, destruction and garbage in our beautiful country? Well, we have cancer, heart disease, diabetes and a whole host of other diseases with more likely on the horizon. Remember the Indians had no diseases when our country was clean and pure; and *we wonder what we are doing wrong?*

God made man from the dirt and dust of the earth and it was clean and pure which was good. Man was all natural but if God returned today and made man from the dirt and dust of the earth many would probably be part beer can, part plastic bottle, part plastic bag and may very well have an old rubber tire for his waist.

We should live within the earth and the earth should live within us. Stop living off the earth like parasites, taking everything and giving nothing in return.

There is no big secret to becoming healthy and free from current diseases; common sense tells me we simply need to clean up Mother Earth and her environment by getting rid of the chemicals and preservatives being added to our food and water. As long as we keep living on an unclean earth and keep eating and drinking all these impurities we are going to keep on being sick; and *we wonder what we are doing wrong?*

As a youngster working in the cotton and corn fields, I went to the creek to bathe at the end of the day and came out of the cold water amazed at how good I felt. Have you ever noticed how much better your car runs and feels after it has been washed and cleaned up? Doesn't it make sense that if we cleaned the earth up that we just might feel the same effect?

Our society no longer seems to love this country nor our neighbors and sometimes not even our own families. We have lost respect for decency as money is now our heart's biggest desire and people will do anything to get it. There is no such thing as a fair price for a good product anymore; it's just an ungodly price for a piece of junk.

It is possible to get our country cleaned up and healthy again and back on the right track but it would take at least ninety percent of the people working toward that goal. It would require strong demands on our government to start doing things right. Will it ever happen? The chances are very slim and why not? We have become accustomed to a lifestyle that is destructive to the earth and we are a greedy people looking out only for ourselves and still; *we wonder what we are doing wrong?*

Preachers tell us the end of time is near and they may be right, but then again, they may not be as only God knows the time for that to happen. Personally I don't believe God has a set time to destroy the earth but that our actions and sins worldwide will determine that time. Hopefully we don't think that just because we have become so bad in this country that it will determine when the entire earth will be destroyed, but if we keep traveling the same path we are now on with our morals continuing to deteriorate and things keep getting worse that He will destroy this country but not the entire earth just as He has done before. It could happen through disease, war or any other number of ways.

40

Like others, I, too, like to store up treasures; but my treasures are not money, wealth or riches. My treasures are the memories of growing up in this great country. God blessed me in many ways choosing to give me two of the best women ever put on the earth and that is the greatest gift ever given to man. They left me with enough good memories from those two marriages to last me for the rest of my life so I plan to keep living with those good memories and if I lose sight of who I am, all I have to do is walk outside at night and hear God's voice in every hoot owl call, in every whippoorwill, bullfrog and even in the old hound dog that's barking up a tree in the distance.

Looking toward heaven I see His face in every star that shines, in the moon and even walking across the Milky Way. I feel His presence with the smell of honeysuckle, in every locust bloom and every other sweet fragrance He put on the earth. In those moments the feeling comes over me that it's just God and me.

My body contains more white man's blood than it does Indian blood but God put a Native American Indian heart in my body and maybe that is why I love this country so much. I respect this land; it is our Mother Earth and to me, it is sacred ground. I want to see this country clean and pure once again so future generations will be able to live and survive here and not have to wonder: *"What are we doing wrong?*

The American Way of Life – Going— Going—Soon to Be Gone

Some folks can recall when life was simple and most people were happy; a time when everyone knew their kinfolk and all their neighbors and found joy in visiting with them. Neighbors were always there to lend a helping hand if any needed help. People gathered on front porches to visit at the end of the work day. Some can even remember when the rivers, lakes and creeks were clean and beautiful; so clean that one could drink from them and there was no litter along our roadways.

41

During those times entire families worked to help make a living, including young children. How thankful I am to God for allowing me to grow up during that period of time.

It was a rare sight to see anyone who was overweight. People ate right and worked the weight off. They didn't run to the doctor all the time because there wasn't a lot of sickness and when we were sick, our parents had a natural remedy to treat us.

The earth was treated with respect because we knew it gave life to us and the food we ate. We knew God gave it to us to live upon and He wanted His people to be happy; and we were.

Back then, I could walk into the woods, sit on a log and listen to the sounds of nature. There was no intrusion from the sounds of automobiles on the roads, air conditioners or heat pumps running, airplanes or outboard motors; just the sounds of Mother Nature. That was the most peaceful sound and it overwhelmed me with peace and joy in my heart.

Then came progress; higher education, fast cars, fast food restaurants, televisions, computers and greedy people seeking that almighty dollar. Things would never be the same again but they now call this the good life.

Remember when God was still allowed in school and the principal and teachers had the authority to discipline misbehaving students? Our government stepped in and took all that away. Now we have a law enforcement officer patrolling schools to keep order. Is this the American way? I don't think so.

If this is the good life, please tell me what's good about greedy oil companies raising gas prices anytime they choose? It is not because there is a shortage; nor because of hurricanes. It is because they project profits into billions of dollars each year and they will reach that goal regardless of how high gas prices go to reach it.

The pharmaceutical companies are just as greedy as the oil companies. It is not a health care organization but a money making operation to produce the pills everyone seems to think they have to take. Have you ever looked at the side effects on the medicines you take? Oftentimes they are worse than the illness.

It's a crying shame that the elderly in this country have been put on so much medicine that many must choose between buying food or medicine. They worked hard to make this country great but are now simply pushed aside. Is this the American way?

The Cancer Society is an organization I have a strong dislike for having had two wives who died from cancer. My first wife died with the help of radiation and chemotherapy and my second wife died strictly from radiation and chemotherapy because at her death, the cancerous tumor in her hip had not grown at all. They could have created a cure for cancer years ago but there is too much money poured into these treatments and organizations and greedy people will not give up that kind of money.

They tell us they don't know what causes cancer—Bull! Common sense tells us that what we eat, drink, and breathe causes it. As a kid we never heard of anyone dying from cancer so what is different now than then? Everything we consume has chemicals that are not good for our bodies.

We can no longer buy anything at the grocery store that is free from chemicals of some kind. It's a difficult task to eat right in America. If we could find truly organically grown vegetables, fruits, meats, milk and eggs that would be a big plus but many so-called organic foods have been found to contain chemicals too.

It appears to me that we are using up all the natural raw materials the earth has to offer as fast as we can without regard for the future. They say our children are our future but how will their children live on the earth after it's been stripped of its raw materials and fresh water has all been poisoned beyond use? I don't' believe that is the American way.

A majority of Americans are overweight and Alabama is near the top in the statistics. It's no secret that overweight causes health problems.

Even our churches are different now. It seems as if each church tries to outdo the other by building huge facilities costing millions of dollars while they collect monies to send to foreign missions. I believe that somewhere in the Bible God tells us to take care of our own and yes, we do have Americans who go hungry every day!

Native American Indians know poverty and hunger more than any others in America but they are forgotten and have been since the day they were put on reservations. God has not forgotten them. Their rewards will come in heaven and I hope God will forgive the white people for what they have done and are still doing to them.

Why can't we Americans do things right? We live in the greatest country in the world but make so many mistakes. Why can't we take care of Mother Earth, love one another and have joy and happiness in our hearts?

This essay is just my opinion and I don't mean to offend anyone. Besides, who am I to know the answers to America's problems? I didn't finish high school because my senior year was spent serving at the front lines in Korea trying to help keep the American way of life.

My Hooky Days

My earlier school days were pretty good, managing to make passing grades; I wasn't real smart because my mind roamed and wasn't focused on my books. A happy kid must let their mind roam a little bit.

One beautiful, warm and sunny morning on my walk to school (about sixth grade) with the birds singing their hearts out I just knew the fish would be biting good.

Just over the hill from our house was a large culvert underneath Highway 72 with a deep ditch that ran down to Dement Creek so I came up with a bright idea. I eased off down into the ditch, headed for the creek and went fishing! Skipping school just this one time wouldn't hurt a thing, right?

The next morning was like the day before and even though knowing I had to go to school, however, approaching that ditch once more just couldn't be passed up. It was as if something pulled me back and down into that ditch. So there I went, back down to the creek all the while telling myself that this is it—the last time I will skip school. Tomorrow for sure I would be in school.

In the afternoon, I had to keep my eyes on the sun to tell about the time school was dismissed so then I eased back up into the ditch and headed for home. You guessed it! The next day I wound up back on the creek bank again instead of in school.

William McElyea had dropped out of the school the previous year so he met me at the creek and headed for the river. Supposing I had lucked upon one of the greatest ideas of my life, what could have been any better? Not having to be at school or working in the fields but staying on the river all day—hey, this is the life!

Sometimes my daddy plowed the fields next to the ditch so great care had to be taken. Richard McElyea joined us on our field trips as time when on. He had been in school and surely he felt like he had missed out on the fun.

Now the three of us were not getting much book learning but we were getting educated in the ways of nature and we surely knew how to catch fish. We could have survived if we had ever gotten lost in the forest. Tom Sawyer and Huckleberry Finn had nothing on us; we had fun and enjoyed life for over a month but one day the truant officer showed up at my house.

She asked my mom, "Why has Dale not been coming to school?"

Mom stood up and said, "I will have you know that Dale has been going to school every day, and you need to be out checking on kids that are not!" But, she finally convinced my mom that I had not been in school for some time.

When I got home that afternoon, mom was waiting for me. She wanted to know where I had been all day. I told her I had been at school but saw right off that was a big mistake—I had done said the wrong thing.

After a good whipping and a good talking to, she marched me off to school the next day and it was the most embarrassing time of my life. Our principal, Mr. B. L. Rich, appeared to be about ten feet tall. He walked with authority and one had no doubt who was in charge of school.

When we heard him walk down the hallways at Clements High School, the only sound coming from any classroom was dead silence. He must have liked me a lot that day because I had to stay right by his side all day long.

He led me around by the hair of my head and must have hauled me into every classroom in the entire school, making a prime example of me as to why no one would ever want to play hooky from his school. That was the longest school day of my life.

Still sitting right beside him when the bell rang to dismiss school, he didn't say a word so I started to slowly ease out of my chair. He looked over at me through those heavy eyebrows of his and revealed a hint of a smile across his face. My feelings walking out of school that day were like someone walking out of Folsom Prison.

Needless to say, I never played hooky again. Years later I realized that Mr. Rich had probably done me one of the biggest favors of my life. It was a major wake up call.

The Days of Castor Oil & Outhouses

Young and living at home, in the early spring, our parents believed we needed to do certain things to stay healthy all year. My dad dug sassafras roots in the fall and let them dry all winter and in early spring Mom boiled them to make sassafras tea. Sweetened with honey it was very tasty and good blood medicine.

Next Mom got the bottle of castor oil down and announced it was time for a big dose. Hearing that, I pulled an Elvis and left the building. The next house up the road belonged to Aunt Flora and Uncle Jim Rose and I crawled underneath the floor of their house as far as possible requiring three people to pull me out; my brother Jimmy, my sister Marion and Aunt Odell, Mom's sister.

Aunt Flora stopped whatever she was doing to come and watch this big event. Being a pretty good scrapper, it was not an easy task to get me out from underneath the floor and back home because I fought the whole way. Aunt Flora said this was better than going to the county fair and I can still hear in my mind the way she laughed and carried on.

Once I was drug back home, Mom, with a very stern look of authority, stood on the back porch with a big bottle of castor oil in one hand and a big long switch in the other. Somehow I got a dose of castor oil and whipping at the same time. They came together in my mind but never got smart enough to realize that if I had just taken my medicine I could have avoided the whipping.

Our outhouse was just a one-holer as we had not advanced the ladder of success enough to rate a two-holer. It was a busy place during those spring days and thank God for the dual purpose Sears and Roebuck catalog. When the new one arrived in the mail, the old one went to the outhouse and it was surely better than those old corncobs. You might say that our outhouse functioned as a toiler, a library and a wasp nest.

About that time, the poke sallet had popped up and was big enough to pick a mess. We had three or four messes in the early spring as my parents believed it was good for our health and sometimes had the same effect as castor oil; but I loved poke sallet then and still do.

If we ever coughed or sneezed in the winter, Mom came out with a mustard or pine tar plaster. She pinned it on our long handle underwear over our chest at night and it sure opened us up. There was always the ever popular black draught tea if we needed any relief during the year.

Mom and Dad came from the old school believing in the use of natural remedies to prevent various types of sickness. The Bible tells us that and the older I get the more it assures me that they were right because I don't remember any of us being sick much.

Sometimes I wonder if there are still mothers today who give their kids a dose of castor oil in early spring. If not, all I can say is they are missing out on one big blowout!

Christmas

Christmas was a very special time during my growing up years beginning just a few days before December 25th when we went into the fields in search of the right cedar tree. After the perfect tree was found we brought it home, put a stand on it and took it into the house where the aroma filled our home with the smell of Christmas.

Decorating the tree called for popping popcorn to string with sewing thread which we then wound around and around the tree. We colored sheets of paper, cut them into strips and glued them together to form a chain which was then wrapped around the tree. The final decoration was made by pulling plugs from cotton and placing them randomly on the tree.

Once the tree was decorated, Mom got busy baking cakes and pies which always included a coconut cake, a jam cake, a yellow cake with chocolate icing, a white cake with caramel icing and sometimes a cake made with hickory or walnut goodies in the icing. My favorite pies were coconut and sweet potato and Dad's favorite was egg custard.

The table was spread with these sweets during the Christmas holiday, covered with a tablecloth. What a treat to have a piece of pie or cake whenever you wanted one. Believe me; I took advantage of this opportunity because it was the only time of the year you could do this in our home. If you wanted something different you might try your neighbor's house because they had the same tradition. Aunt Flora's kitchen table was one of my favorite spot to check out.

Christmas Eve was one of the longest days of my life. It seemed as though nightfall would never come and I was always ready to go to bed early that night. My socks were hung over the footboard on my bed then I crawled in and tried to stay awake until Santa Claus came. For some reason I never got to see him though I really wanted to.

The biggest thrill of my life was waking up on Christmas morning to find my socks filled with apples, oranges, nuts and hard candy. "How can Santa Claus be so good to one young boy?" I wondered.

Two Christmas' were very special to me because I received a Gene Autry cap pistol for one and a Lone Ranger cap pistol for the other. Boy, I really loved old Santa Claus after that.

Christmas was the happiest time of the year for me and there were no gifts exchanged really—only a few goodies for the children. Sometimes someone sent a pie or cake over but it was just a happy time for the neighborhood. It was made joyous by everyone visiting with each other—gifts would have spoiled it all.

Back then everybody knew what Christmas was all about—a time to honor and be thankful for the birth and life of our Savior, Jesus Christ. Everyone celebrated this in their own way but it was mostly just good people with good hearts giving praises to the One that provided it all. I know I thanked Him a bunch for my cap pistols.

There was a lot of love among the people in our community. They cared for one another and if any family was down on their luck and needed help, they never had to ask—it just always showed up. We were poor but happy folk, thankful for what we had.

Although my youthful Christmas times were the happiest and most joyful, now they are some of my saddest times. Losing my two wives to cancer is one reason and knowing what was done to Jesus on the cross is another but I don't understand all the reasons why but one other reason in our history comes to mind. It was the Great Emancipator, Abraham Lincoln, who on the day after Christmas gave the order for America's greatest mass execution as thirty eight Native Americans were hanged for fighting for their homeland.

Now it seems that almost everyone has forgotten the true meaning of the day. Most see it as a time to spend a lot of money going head over heels into debt to buy gifts for people who for the most part dislike them and end up in return lines the next day.

Wouldn't it be great if people would give up part of their shopping time to get reacquainted with kinfolk and neighbors? You never know; they might be some good people and you might even get the true spirit of Christmas.

Christmas is a giving time of year to me as I love to give gifts and I'm not opposed to others giving either but to me, finding a family in need, filling a box with food and delivering it to them is what it's about. When you see the look in their faces, then you can know what Christmas is all about and it is even more special if you keep it between you and the good Lord.

Being a little old-fashioned in this modern world, I believe that God is the same today as He was thousands of years ago. Could it be He is a little old-fashioned too?

The greatest gift anyone can give or receive on Christmas doesn't cost a dime. It is a simple four letter word called **LOVE.** So to everyone I wish for you a very happy and safe Christmas holiday. May it be the merriest ever and may you receive many gifts and I'll see you the day after in the return line.

Remembering My First Girlfriend

My basketball career began when I entered the seventh grade. Just before the start of my ninth grade court career, a party was held at school celebrating the start of the new season. It was there I noticed a little blond girl—about the prettiest girl I had ever seen.

Bashful as ever I finally worked up enough nerve to approach her and speak. Standing there looking into Marjorie Tribble's beautiful eyes, my heart melted. Bravely I asked, "Can I walk you home after the party?" Her reply was, "I will let you know." My eyes followed her the rest of the evening and each time she caught me looking at her, she smiled back. Imagine my delight when she later told me that I could walk her home; overjoyed was an understatement.

We held hands as we walked that night. Whether we actually did much talking or not I cannot remember but I experienced feelings inside me never before felt. As we approached her front door, less than a mile from school, she stepped up to the doorstep and turned facing me. "What am I supposed to do now?" I wondered. It was my first time ever but I took a chance and kissed her lightly on the lips. We said goodnight and I headed home, my heart pumping like an old John Deere tractor all fired up. Walking on Cloud Nine all the way home, I had to be the happiest boy in the entire world. It was later that I discovered she had changed her plans to spend the night with a girlfriend just so she could walk home with me. She liked me and it really felt great.

After that night you could say that went steady though she didn't have much chance to go with anyone else. Marjorie was my first girlfriend and this Alabama boy had stuck gold!

Marjorie was a cheerleader so with me being on the team, we made a good pair. On game days I walked to her house and we walked together from there to the school. Because she was there cheering me on, I played hard, always trying to impress her which probably contributed to my success as a good basketball player.

We rode the bus together to the away games and that was quite nice. After the game, she hurried to the bus to get us a good seat near the back allowing us to hug and kiss whenever we could. A very happy couple, we both enjoyed the basketball games because it allowed us to spend time together. Compliments on my basketball abilities was nice, however, a bigger thrill came when compliments about us being a good looking couple came.

We improved greatly and had a great season that year winning most of our games. God blessed me with the a talent on the court and the best looking girl in the school as my girlfriend and I often remembered to thank Him for being so good to me.

Once the season ended, Marjorie and her mother moved about two miles from the school but still within walking distance to see her. Some of the boys had cars and I knew my chances of holding onto her grew slim because walking those old dirt and gravel roads couldn't hold much appeal to a girl when she could ride in style.

We shared a happy and special time in my life and I will always treasure the memories as her sweetheart and best friend. A year ahead of me in school, she and her family moved to Detroit after she graduated. My senior year was spent on the front lines in Korea and while there received the news that Marjorie had married someone in Detroit—but life goes on. Though we both moved on, those fond memories will always hold a dear spot in my heart.

The Class of 1951

The war in Korea broke out in 1950. The first year Clements High had a football team. Four boys were prepared to start their senior year, William McElyea and I played sports while the other two, Richard McElyea and Harry Kerr were involved in other activities.

The four of us had grown up together as the best of friends hunting, fishing and camping out on the banks of the Elk River. We four friends stayed close even after courting and dating began. We all had to work to help make a living as our parents were poor folks but that never stopped us from enjoying life.

At sixteen years of age we each decided to join the National Guard Unit in Athens and were assigned to Company B of the 1343rd Combat Engineer Unit. It was a way for us to earn extra money aside from chopping and picking cotton. It worked out pretty well for a while with our first training in 1949 at Fort Benning, Georgia for two weeks.

However, during the summer of 1950 while William, Harry and I were practicing football and Richard was busy with other activities, our battalion was mobilized into active service—we became official military members and our lives changed forever.

Our training began at the fairgrounds in Athens though, as time allowed we continued to practice football. We actually got to play our first game on the field at Athens High School since Clements didn't have a football field yet. Our team played Tanner High School and took a good lickin' from the Tanner boys.

The following Saturday, the four of us boarded a troop train bound for Fort Campbell, Kentucky for basic training. After that we boarded another troop train headed west. About a week later we pulled into Seattle, Washington—and it does rain a lot there. After a few days we got a pass to go into town and listened to a particular song that would be forever played in our minds; *The Tennessee Waltz* by Patti Page. Of course it made us ole country boys homesick.

Next we boarded the ship *The Marine Phoenix* one evening unsure of our destination. We bunked for the night and awoke the next morning with some of us experiencing seasickness.

About a month later we docked in Yokohama, Japan where we stayed for less than a day. The crew didn't know their destination was Korea until the following day. The ship docked again in Pusan, Korea and within a few weeks the necessary equipment had been gathered in preparation for war. The battalion headed north travelling through Inchon and Seoul, cities completely destroyed by bombs. As we travelled further north, we began to hear the big guns firing and each of us knew our exact destination.

Reminiscing, we talked about our class back home and wondered how it would have been to be back in school, however, we never once complained about our circumstances. We knew it was our duty to perform any task our superiors commanded.

We left Athens as boys but became men in Korea as our love for family and country grew stronger. We each had a new perspective of freedom and got on speaking terms with the Good Lord. That was our strength as we continued in the worst of circumstances but held hope for the future.

After thirteen months in Korea, we left for home as proud Americans and took pride in our ability to serve our country. We learned more about life in Korea than we could have ever learned in school and left Korea walking tall and proud.

Our families welcomed us home and were happy for our safe return, however it seemed that no one really understood what we had experienced and lived. No one truly knew the cost of the war and gratitude was not expressed by the public. Freedom was taken for granted.

If the truth be known there is likely no other U. S. school that had twenty five percent of its senior class removed, sent to war and return home alive! Could this be a record for our little county school in Athens Alabama?

As one of those four young men, I can honestly say that I am proud to have served with Richard, William and Harry. It was an honor and I thank each of you for serving our country in an unselfish manner. I love each of you as my brothers and you are among my heroes.

The Soldier

Americans today have one of the greatest rewards ever bestowed upon people living on this earth—freedom. That freedom didn't come from the President of the United States, the Congress nor law enforcement. It came from the soldier.

In America we can go to the church of our choice, worship God anyway we please, go into our closets to pray or walk into the woods, look to heaven and worship God. It is not the preacher, the pastor, the priest or rabbi who gives us this choice. It is the soldier.

We can travel anywhere in this country, live anywhere in America we choose and come and go as we please. It is not the travel agent or automobile manufacturer who gives us this privilege. It is the soldier.

We can run this country down, burn the flag, talk badly about the leaders of this nation and still walk the streets free—although a soldier may want to shoot anyone for burning the flag—but still, it is the soldier who gives us the freedom to this.

What percentage of Americans were soldiers? My guess would be no more than ten percent. If this is the case then about ninety percent of our citizens do not realize the cost of freedom. That majority cannot comprehend what the soldier goes through. Freedom is not free. The cost is monumental and who pays? It is the soldier.

In my opinion the soldier is the least respected person in America, second only to the Native American Indian. Since the 911 tragedy, soldiers get more respect than before. If young people today have heroes they are probably ball players, movie stars or rock singers. There will never be a greater hero than the soldier—maybe that is the only real hero.

Native American Indians gave us the food we seem to overly enjoy. The American soldier gave us the freedom we take for granted so it's not by chance that at Indian festivals and Powwows they give more honor and praise to soldiers than anyone else and what an honor it is to be honored by the people I honor.

One day I look forward to going to the Home in the Sky because heaven will be blessed with many soldiers and Indians. What a festival and Powwow that will be! Heaven is where American soldiers and Native Indians will truly be rewarded and honored.

How can we Americans lie in our soft, warm beds at night with peace in our hearts when so many soldiers who fought for our freedom are homeless, living on the streets and eating from garbage cans? How can we pass by them when they sit on the sidewalk with a tin cup; some without hands, feet, arms or legs?

How can our government ignore our veterans when they are in such deep need? They took an oath to protect this country and they did just that but what does our country do for them? Apparently the leaders in Washington who sit in their big, fine offices, smoking their big cigars, drinking their expensive whiskey and collecting money under the table are simply too busy to care.

No, not everything is right in America but we will never find enough people who care enough to do anything about it.

Unsung Heroes

When the 1343rd Combat Engineer Company B left Athens early one morning in August 1950, there were some who had served our country in the military before but there were many of us green kids straight out of the cotton fields. We traveled to Fort Campbell Kentucky where we learned to be soldiers. After completing basic training, we took the long journey to Pusan, Korea.

Upon our arrival in Pusan, we were attached to the 36th Engineer Combat Group where we trained more and worked on projects in and around the area including the United Nations Cemetery, road maintenance and developing supply routes while waiting for the bulk of our equipment to arrive.

Next we boarded LST's and headed toward Inchon by way of the Yellow Sea. Upon our arrival the effects of the war were plainly seen. It was a frightening experience for young boys who should have been home attending high school but we stuck our chests out and appeared brave as we traveled toward the front lines.

Now attached to the 10th Corps, I only recall moving back southward one time. All the rest of the time we moved northward staying close to the front lines. We worked long, hard hours sometimes day and night building roads and keeping them open for our troops. We built bridges during the rainy season when the rivers overflowed the banks;

worked in bitter cold and snow in the winter with temperatures sometimes dropping to forty degrees below zero. We used tons of explosives to blast roads through rocky mountainsides and other projects like building field hospitals for the wounded.

We traveled above the 38th parallel from Inje Pass to the Punch Bowl and did all that was asked of us because we were proud Americans and loved our country. We never wanted anything like that to happen in our homeland. We became more in touch and closer to God and felt His presence near us at all times.

Our battalion commander, Colonel Henry C. Mabry was easily recognized. When he came up in his jeep, we had better stand up and salute him. After a few months there I realized this man was a great leader who cared about his men. He was gentle but possessed great knowledge and authority.

Thinking back to many situations we found ourselves in during our time in North Korea, I realize that it was this man's great leadership ability and care for his troops that kept us from winding up dead lying in a rice paddy.

General Mabry, "It was truly an honor and privilege to have served with a man of your character. Thank you for taking a bunch of green kids and making men and soldiers out of us. You are truly an unsung American hero."

Colonel Mabry accomplished many missions by having great leaders under his command. One that comes to mind is platoon leader Ed McMunn. He was the kind of soldier I wanted to be my leader if I were going into war today. He has my greatest respect and yet today he is more actively helping veterans than anyone I know. He is another unsung hero.

Our company was made up of many great leaders including Commanders Funchess and Proctor, Lieutenants Swanner, Elmore, Shaw and Gossett, First Sergeant Black and many others. A few that I felt closer to include Sergeants McGivney, R. Grigsby, E. Vanhoose and J. Smith. Everyone in our company was a great man and soldier. They deserve more praise than I could ever give and it was an honor to serve with each and every one of them.

On returning home, we were proud of the fact that we had served our country to the best of our ability. We walked tall and held our heads high because we knew what we had endured and accomplished. A simple 'thank you' would have been nice to hear, but that never happened.

Hundreds of thousands of men and women have given their lives for our freedom. Sometimes I wonder how many people realize that. Whenever attending a Memorial Day service or other veteran function, it seems about the only ones to attend are old soldiers with their wives and maybe of few of their children.

When you see someone sitting on the sidewalk with his legs blown off and with a cup of pencils in his hand, don't be too quick to judge. He may have lost his legs in war fighting for your freedom and God may look through his eyes to see how you react or that old wino that gets kicked around on the streets may have gone through such horrific things during war that he simply can't get off the bottle. My God has a special place for soldiers who gave so much for our freedom. In my book all of them are truly the greatest unsung American heroes.

Sunny – Orphaned by the War

The men of Company B were assigned to improve the dirty, muddy road for the U. N. supply routes. SFC James A. McLlwain known to us as Hoss, and his squad of engineers worked on a stretch of road just north of Hongcheon in South Korea one day when they heard weak moans from behind a hedge row adjoining the road.

Upon investigation, Hoss and his men were surprised to find a half starved and nearly dead, little Korean girl. She held a smaller boy in her arms and cried feebly in her fright. Horse surveyed the situation quickly and knew they had found two of the many thousands of abandoned Korean children in the face of the Chinese assault the previous spring.

Sgt. McLlwain aka Hoss contacted the Korean police and was quickly informed that they could do nothing as there were thousands in the same situation and they couldn't perform their duties and take care of every case.

Disgusted, Sgt. McLlwain immediately contacted Lt. Proctor, commander of Company B. He assisted by Lt. Kim, commanding officer of a Korean Labor Company attached to our unit were able to get the story from the trembling, parched lips of this brave six year old girl. Our company adopted her and called her Sunny. Lt. Kim told the following story:

"When the Chinese began their spring offensive, Sunny along with her mother and little brother (age three and a half), started on a long, weary trip southward with many other displaced Koreans. Just north of Chechen, the mother died leaving the two children alone. Not knowing exactly what to do, Sunny became separated from the rest of her people.

"Lost and alone, she decided to go back to her home not realizing it had been destroyed by the Chinese. Carrying her small brother and weak from the lack of food, she started her journey northward and according to her story, traveled day and night following a large river and staying away from the roadside.

"All this time her little brother grew weaker by the hour because she found only meager bits of food. After about a week of living in constant fear, Sunny stopped to rest in the shade of a large tree on the riverbank. By this time her little brother had weakened to the point that he suffered severe hemorrhages of the nose."

It was at that point they were found. She tried to stop the hemorrhaging by stuffing grass up into his nostrils. They were immediately brought to our company area and the battalion doctor, Lt. Joseph Blackshear was called.

He decided the boy was in bad need of medical attention not available in our area so he was taken to a hospital where he died a few days later. Sunny was put on a liquid diet and Sgt. Pat Aday, one of the medics, stayed with her day and night feeding her juice.

Under Sgt. Aday's care, Sunny began to show signs of recovery and before long was well enough to walk. Though he won't tell you, Lt. Kim told Lt. Proctor that Sgt. Aday never once took his eyes off the lifeless face of Sunny as she lay on a straw mat too weak to move.

Her nourishment had to be forced into her mouth as she had no idea what was happening to her. By all appearances new life began for her that night as she had no apparent recollection of anything preceding her rescue. Even her story of her unbelievable trip from Chechen faded from her memory.

To our knowledge she never mentioned her mother or brother although I imagine she wondered where they were. Once Sunny was on the road to recovery, our problem became clothes for her. It being summertime, one of the guys took a GI issued undershirt and came up with a dress and underwear for her.

Sunny considered this a fine replacement for the tattered garment she was found in and of course she was really happy when she opened the first box of clothes she received from Athens. Her eyes were as big as saucers when she saw all those pretty little dresses. Sunny was sincerely thrilled; her expressions alone told the story. She had never before seen clothes like those.

Sunny became one of our big family and always with a smile for each of us. On movie night she was found in the front row taking in the show and on most evenings Sunny showed up to listen to the music as we played records. Though she didn't speak English yet, most of us spoke enough Korean to say a few words to her. She was happy there with us and most loved her like a daughter.

She began to come through the chow line to get something to eat though at first she ate only with the South Korean company but eventually temptation got to her. We didn't blame her because the Koreans ate mostly rice with garlic. She was happy and jolly around us, always smiling.

One day I received pictures from home and showed them to her trying to explain that they were my family. She looked up and smiled but seemed confused. She tried to comprehend what it might be like to live as an American so unlike the way her life had been in Korea.

Because most of us treated her like a daughter, Sunny thought she had one big family now. She was such a joy to have around and the only bright spot about the war. She had the run of the entire company; whatever she wanted to do, somebody saw that she got to do it.

Just before rotation began, the original company took up money for her. We knew she would have to be taken somewhere and taken care of although she wasn't aware of what was about to happen.   An orphanage in Pusan agreed to take her and the money collected was solely for the purpose of her being taken care of there.

When the day for her departure arrived no one in the company knew of it except the commanding officer who informed Rupert McElyea that it was his duty to transport Sunny back to Headquarters and that she was not to know what was going to take place. Rupert was to load her clothes and belongings into the weapons carrier without her knowing it. When he finished that he went to look for her. He found her in the mess hall and said, "Come on Sunny. Let's go riding."

She was all for that because she had been riding with him a lot when he checked on the South Koreans and even went with him to get food supplies for the laborers. She hopped into the vehicle all smiles but she happened to look into the weapons carrier and saw her clothes so she jumped back out.

Here was a child who had lost her home, mother and brother within the past few months. She thought she had found a new family but I don't believe she ever thought that we might go back to our home someday. Now she was losing another family she had grown to love very much. As she stood by the jeep with tears running down her little face, she was not the only one with tears falling from their eyes.

Rupert had to summon Kim Yung Ho to come and talk to her. How could anyone talk to a little girl who was so upset, sobbing and heartbroken? Sunny had known more sadness and hurt in her short life than most will know in a lifetime and Kim talked to her for a long time, convincing her that she would have a better life in a home with children her own age.

Finally Kim picked her up in his arms, got into the vehicle and held her as they drove away. Except for the sobbing of the little girl, it was a quiet ride. Someone was waiting at Headquarters Company to pick her up but I'm sure it was a hard task for Rupert although he was the only one in our company who got to hug Sunny and tell her goodbye.

The amount of money taken up for her I'll never know but when they returned, Rupert made a comment that Sunny was likely the richest little girl in Korea.

One of the saddest days in Korea was when we came in from work that day and heard the news that Sunny was gone. It was quiet as hardly anyone spoke and not much supper was eaten that night. We had lost the only ray of sunshine in our daily lives and it was not a good day. We didn't understand why we weren't allowed the opportunity to tell her goodbye.

Bedtime came early that night; there was no reason to stay up as Sunny wouldn't pop into our tents with that big smile anymore. All I could think of was little Sunny as I lay there that night with tears running down my face. That little girl touched the heart of every man in our company and it was amazing.

My Dream Came True

On my arrival in Korea in early 1951, my senior high school class had had already begun. Joining the National Guard at sixteen, our unit was mobilized in August 1950 just before the start of school although I was able to play in one football game before deployment.

When I left to go overseas, I had a girlfriend from another school but it wasn't long after arriving in Korea before receiving a 'Dear John' letter. Hurt and a little sad, I began to draw an image in my mind of a beautiful girl and after a few weeks it was perfected.

During my time in Korea, this imaginary girl was foremost in my mind knowing that someday we would meet. The winters were harsh and bitterly cold—sometimes as cold as forty degrees below zero but just thinking about my lady made me feel warm all over and I felt good. She was the thing that gave me hope and a reason to keep going; I had fallen very much in love with her.

Two days after Christmas in 1951, walking guard duty on a ridge on the backside of our camp, it was thirty something below zero and snow was knee deep; just a miserable night in the Punch Bowl. Many soldiers died in that place but I had my lady on my mind. In my mind, we were in a log cabin with a fire burning in the fireplace—it was so cozy and warm as we sipped a glass of wine. Holding my imaginary lady in my arms she said, "We will be together some day." And I believed we would.

After returning home to the states I began to look for my dream girl, looking for months and then giving up hope of finding her when one night I met a girl named Willene White. She was still in high school and we dated for a couple of years, and married in 1956. I loved her very much and we shared thirty three years together before she died of cancer. She was as good a person as I have ever known.

About two years before she passed away, the two of us were at a meeting in Birmingham, Alabama. We sat down behind a couple and the lady turned around to speak to us. When she did I looked into the face of my dream girl. Nearly falling out of my seat, I asked God why He let that happen then. I couldn't take my eyes off her that day but knew I had to let her go the same day I found her. We were both married.

Willene and I became good friends with this woman and her husband but I knew it could never be anything but friendship and that's all it was until Willene lost her life. Soon after that my dream girl's husband filed for divorce and it was then we started seeing each other.

Jo and I were married on December 27, 1991 exactly forty years after my dream or vision in the Punch Bowl. Following the wedding we were invited to eat dinner where we stayed that night. It was very nice as we had the whole dining room to ourselves except for the band which played romantic music. It was then that I finally told Jo about having her with me on those cold and lonely nights in Korea and I knew she believed me when tears rolled down her cheeks.

She said, "I will love you forever," and she did. She died in August 2000. God has blessed me with so much and yet I have lost so much.

The Korean War Valor Flight

Back in 1952 when we began arriving back home from the Korean War, our families welcomed us and thanked us for fighting for our country; but outside our families we didn't receive any recognition or thanks from anyone else.

The four of us high school boys never heard from any of our classmates nor anyone else from our school while in Korea. After arriving back home our school never honored or recognized us but that was okay because we knew what we had done, what we had been through and were proud of it. Maybe they didn't realize what it was like to be in a war.

In 2011, my friend Richard McElyea heard about sending Korean War veterans to Washington DC on an honor flight to see the Korean Monument so he signed us up. Having never been recognized before I didn't think there would be much to it.

We went to Huntsville for orientation a few weeks before the scheduled flight and after processing was completed they spoke to us about what to expect when we arrived. Each veteran was to have a guardian with them at all times. They said, "You veterans will be treated like celebrities." "Yeah," I thought, "that's a joke—there might be a few people at the airport."

On November 12th, we arrived at the Huntsville Airport at 5:00 A. M. and to my surprise there was a large crowd, an Army band played music and a gentleman who played the bagpipes. Three Star General Richard Formica, whom we had met the week before at the Veteran's Museum breakfast, was there and so was Eric Sollmon, Channel 48 newscaster. They were to accompany us on the flight. There was a total of one hundred and ten veterans and most of our guardians (some met their guardians in Washington including me) as well as the Valor Flight Group, paramedics and the gentleman with the bagpipes.

Leaving the airport, the pilot announced that our arrival would be in one hour and twenty minutes. My opinion of Washington and the people there wasn't too high because I based my feelings on my experience and knowledge of government and politicians in general. After landing and disembarking I got the surprise of my life.

A huge crowd greeted us and they were some of the friendliest and most caring people I've ever met. The Valor Flight Group was right—they did treat us like celebrities. It took some time to find my guardian but he finally showed up having gone to the wrong airport. "Yeah, I'm going to have a great time with this guy," I thought but he later told me he had to drive about a hundred miles an hour to get to the right airport.

Busses waited to take us from one destination to another with our first stop being the Korean War Monument. What an amazing sight. Many memories rushed back about my days in Korea. For all our brothers who didn't make it back home, I believe each one of us said a silent prayer for them. Arlington National Cemetery was a sobering sight; also the changing of the guards at the Tomb of the Unknown Soldier. It was an honor to see the gravesite of my hero Audie Murphy and the Marine Monument of the Iwo Jima flag raising touched me because of my Indian brother Ira Hayes.

My guardian, Carl Williamson, quickly became my good friend. Someone asked him about the bag he had on his back and he told them, "I got drinks, chips, candy . . . " and he jokingly added other things like lipstick. As we walked and talked later I said, "Carl, you know when I signed up for this flight I asked for a young beautiful girl for my guardian. And what did they give me—a black man who carries lipstick in his bag." He cracked up.

The people in Washington DC were the first ones to give us any kind of recognition for going to war. Until we arrived back in Huntsville, I guess the people in Alabama just couldn't bring themselves to do that. After sixty years, the crowd that jammed into the airport made a bunch of old soldiers feel like they had come home again.

My thanks I give to the president of Valor Flight, Mr. Steve Celuch and his group. Many hours of work and planning go into an event like this and I am eternally grateful. My thanks also go to the paramedics who traveled with us and to General Richard Formica for his support. Thank you to the gentleman who played the bagpipes and to Eric Sollmon and Channel 48 News for making the trip, too. In Eric I feel like I have a new friend. Thank you to the children at Lynn Fanning Elementary School also for the notes and colored pictures. They were great.

Thank you to anyone who had anything to do with this trip. Korea may have been the forgotten war, but we old veterans never forgot. What was done for us on November 12, 2011 filled a sixty year void in our hearts. Thank you and God bless America.

Alabama Ramblers

Some of the 1343rd Battalion left for overseas taking their musical instruments with them, mostly for our own entertainment. Once we arrived in Korea, some talked about getting a band together so Jerry McGivney took hold of the reins and lined everyone up.

Jerry had a difficult time getting everyone together for practice because this 'music thing' could not interfere with our regular duties. Fortunately, he never gave up and practice began what was to become a group known as *The Alabama Ramblers;* which never would have existed without his persistence. Because he was such a nice guy, he held many titles in the band including manager, booking agent, driver and master of ceremonies.

It wasn't long before our group recorded tapes and mailed them back home to Bob Dunnavant at radio station WJMW in Athens Bob was a good friend to the band and played our music including the recorded messages on the tapes for our families

We performed many shows in a variety of places and really enjoyed entertaining. It appeared the band and the music were truly loved by the crowds. However, we were the only show in town so it was *The Alabama Ramblers* or nothing.

Occasionally our young band performed at field hospitals where the patients and nurses treated us like big stars. Our group knew we had touched a heart when tears were seen rolling down one's cheek. Perhaps the music and words caused one to reminisce of loved ones or home and for a brief moment forget about the dangers lurking around them. We were always welcomed and it wasn't difficult to gather a good crowd no matter where we performed as everyone was hungry for any type of entertainment. Often we returned back to camp late at night or early the next morning but still had to fall out like the rest of the soldiers and perform our assigned duties.

Perhaps the group wasn't a 'Great Band' but there were some great entertainers in it. J. W. Hudson sang the number he wrote, *Away from You*; it always went over well. The Proctor Brothers, Stan White and Robert 'Catfish' Allen, were very good singers also. Richard McElyea and Charles Adams always had good performances while Fred B. Clem, the mandolin picker and comedian, kept everyone laughing.

Robert Grigsby played a mean harmonica and James Price, the old boy from Missouri, played steel guitar. George Naope, the only professional among us, had a band or orchestra back home in Hawaii and had performed in one of Bing Crosby's movies.

Eventually Hank Williams heard the tapes that had been sent to the radio station and the group heard that Hank liked their music and wanted them to appear on his show at the Grand Ole Opry. However, before the men returned home, Hank was fired from the Opry and died shortly afterwards.

Kneeling, left to right: PFC Stanley White, Hartselle; MSgt Jerry McGivney, Athens; PFC George Naope, Hilo Hawaii; Sgt 1ˢᵗ Class J. W. Hudson, Athens, Sgt. Richard McElyea, Athens.
Standing left to right: MSgt Dee Proctor, Hartselle; MSgt Howard Proctor, Hartselle; Sgt Robert M. Allen, Sgt Charles Adams and CPL Fred B. Clem all of Athens; PFC James Price, Owensville, MO; Sgt Robert Grigsby and CPL Dale Casteel also of Athens.

Members of *The Alabama Ramblers* really enjoyed performing possibly touching a few hearts, made a few people happy and helped them all forget about the war for a moment. If we did that then all the work and time was worth it.

It was with pride that I was a small part of the band. We served our country with pride and honor and our music made a few people smile.

Just maybe somewhere across America, someone who served in Korea during that time can recall the old country band from North Alabama called *The Alabama Ramblers* and smile.

Three Little Indians

There were three young braves that grew up together in the same village. We were half-breed Indian braves; our names were Qui Ha Di, pronounced Kwe Ha De; Wi Li Ha Ma, pronounced We Lee Ha Ma and De Li, pronounced Day Lee. We never cared much for white man's school for to us it was a waste of valuable time. We braves were big hunters and fishermen. We loved living outside on river bank or in woods hunting for food. We very good at doing this. Very close friends growing up. Indian blood in our veins attracted us to be blood brothers. We very close to nature. Sometimes talk to animals; outdoors our home.

In sixth grade Wi Li Ha Ma decided white man's school was not for him so he drop out. De Li come up with big plan. He began to play hooky from white man's school. De Li meet up with Wi Li Ha Ma; head to river, fish all day. Two days pass. Qui Ha Di find out, then join us on big adventure. We three smartest braves in white man's school. What better than fish all day long every day? We plenty smart; can tell time by sun. We leave river; get home right after school let out.

Here three braves that outsmart elders and entire white man's school system. We often laugh and talk about dumbbell kids. They sit in hot classrooms all day long. We get good education; nature teach us. We learn from wild animals and birds. We become smart Indian braves. We sure our expedition can last forever. We coast along as free as birds. After one moon, we think we are great warriors of forest. We had no fear living without advice from elders but one day big change come.

Walk into my lodge one day feeling on top of mountain. My mother ask, Where you been all day?" Me answer, "School." I see right off say wrong thing. In her eyes, Cherokee Indian blood begin to boil.

She say to me, "You almost have me ready to kill that darned old woman from schoolhouse. She tell me you no come to school. I tell her you go to school every day; almost smack her jaws before she convince me you no go to school. You lay out every day. Now ready to do more than smack your jaws." Thought she going to scalp me."

Took punishment like a young Indian brave; was marched to school next morning. Find out later Qui Ha Di came into same situation at his lodge. That school day was most humiliating and embarrassing day for young Indian brave. Principal was heap big man, maybe seven feet tall. This day he reminded me of very large Apache warrior Geronimo. He lead me around all day by hair on my head; think he going to scalp me without using knife. He make big example of me. No one play hooky from his school ever again. When leave schoolhouse that day, have less hair. Feel like just got out of stockade.

Wi Li Ha Ma return to white man's school. We grew to age of sixteen years, come up with big plan. We join National Guard. Now we make big money, maybe spend on girlfriends. We now ready to go into last year of high school but big change come. They say U. S. Army need young braves to go to Korea to help win war. Army know we good hunters. Know how to use guns and tomahawk. In 1950, only good thing no more white man's school. We take basic training. We learn fast. Make good soldiers.

1951 we land in Korea. Get off big boat after coming across big river. Never before see so much water. While class was finishing high school, three young braves were at frontlines. We chase North Koreans and Chinese all over big mountains in North Korea. Those little yellow devils had never seen three wild Indians with tomahawks doing war dance. They run fast. Not like to stop and fight. Not afraid. We do what head chief say. Now come time to get on big boat to go home.

Family glad to see us home; others ungrateful for young warriors serving our country. We not upset. We know we do good job. We served with honor and pride.

We now elders. Very happy Creator gave us good lives. My great friends Qui Ha Di and Wi Li Ha Ma have been following the white man's religion. Very happy for them, but my Indian ancestors had other plans for me. Very happy they helped me choose spiritual ways of my Indian people. Now feel very special closeness to Creator. Let Him lead me on my trail. Path I follow and path my friends follow lead to same place.

Three now old warriors, still live at the present time; in our eighties. Guess it like they say about old Indians, 'They never die; just fade away." I honor my Indian blood brothers.

In the Beginning

When God created this great earth, all living things came from the dirt of this great body. Now if all living things came from this one body, Mother Earth, why would we all not be related to each other as the Indian people believe? If God gave man a spirit, why not all living things having spirits as the Indians believe? If man is the only one with a spirit, will there only be man living in heaven? No trees, no plants, no animals of any kind? If only man goes to the city with the streets paved with gold, it seems heaven would all be a desert except for the cities. Forgive me but I don't see this as being heaven. God, You had better watch the white men like a hawk with the streets paved with gold, one day they will come up missing.

In my heart God lets me see heaven as the most beautiful place eyes ever laid on. It is a paradise with all green vegetation growing in abundance, every kind of wild animal roaming over prairies and forests, clean rivers, lakes and streams. All things are pure and healthy with all life living in harmony with each other as it was in the beginning of this earth. This makes much more sense to me to live as the Indians believe than to live as non-Indians believe.

When God made man He said, "Let him be in my image. Let him have dominion over every living thing on this earth." God gave man the knowledge and power to do anything he wanted to do, good or bad. When God gave man all this power, He expected him to take care of His creation, but through the years man has lost the will to do this.

Maybe if people in America today could believe more like the Indians, they would not be in such a hurry to cut down all the trees, kill all of the wild animals and use up all the raw materials in this earth.

Maybe if they could look at them as being related to them they would not be in such a rush to kill them.

This is pretty far out for modern man's thinking, but not so much for an Indian. When the Indian first lived in this country, he sure must have had a lot more knowledge than modern man because the Indian's life was filled with happiness, clean waters and earth and free from diseases; and he had the knowledge to keep it that way.

Just maybe God, You could have two heavens, one for Indians and one for everyone else. Just give us a place like this earth was when you first put us here. It was a paradise; we needed nothing more. For non-Indians just give them all the modern things they love. By the way, Lord, please give them all the gold. We had enough trouble with that here on this earth.

Lord, we know You are a just God, so whatever kind of heaven you give to us Indians, we will be forever thankful. We have lived so long with not too much of anything; just to have enough food to eat to keep us from being hungry and enough clothes to keep us warm would make us feel like we were living in a paradise. Just give us a path to our neighbor's house and please, God, no gold on it; just dirt from where we came from will be just fine.

What Does God Think?

Often, I wonder how God feels about the situation here in America and how the way people act. How does He feel about the things our government is doing? Are they doing things He would want us to pray for or is He fed up with them like most of us are?

How does God feel about all the filthy movies and television shows being made and shown for everyone to see, with the raw sex, brutal killings and bad language? It seems to me that decent movies and television programs are a thing of the past.

These movies and programs have become so accustomed to people's lifestyles that most everyone now watches them but I don't believe God wants His people watching that trash. He doesn't want His children to learn more from these programs than they learn in school.

What does He think of the computer and internet, a machine that can expose most everything about anyone? Many children use it to learn about bad things. It may be good in some ways but it is bad in many more.

Sometimes I wonder how God feels about all the different religions that have been created in America. Why do so many have different names on their churches? Most churches use the Bible as their guide but every denomination sees some things a little different in them. Did God mean for it to be this way? Nobody knows for sure though many think they do. Even people in the same church often can't get along. To me, God would like to see buildings with just one name on them "Church" and everyone working together as brothers and sisters to one day meet God.

After attending many different denominational churches and having nothing against any of them, there still is a difference in all of them about how they feel about other churches. God wants us to be brothers and sisters to all people. There is only one race that has the same spiritual beliefs and that is the Native American Indians.

Of all the churches and places I have worshiped my Savior, I feel God's presence more with the Indian gatherings than any other place, so I walk the Red Road and follow the spiritual ways of the Native Indians. They have always worshiped the one Creator the same, and God was good to them. He let them live in this country for thousands of years without any kind of diseases. I sometimes wonder if the people here today would have worshiped the Creator as much as the Indian people did; would we now be living in a better country.

Everyone has their own beliefs about God and His creation and I believe His creation is a sacred place and we as His people need to take care of it instead of destroying it. How does God feel about the shape His creation today? He sends us signs daily to warn us that things are not right in this world.

Thanksgiving

Many Americans just don't understand what Thanksgiving is for, how it came into being and why we celebrate it. There are three important things I remember at this time of the year.

We need to remember and give thanks to the American soldier. They fought and many died for our freedom.

We need to remember and give thanks to the Native American Indians who introduced the Europeans to their first Thanksgiving.

We need to remember God the Creator of all life and thank Him for our bountiful harvest and all the things He blesses us with.

Freedom is not free as many Americans think; it comes at a very high price. Hundreds of thousands of soldiers have given their lives so we can live in freedom. We need to thank them every day for their sacrifice so that our family can gather around the table on Thanksgiving and enjoy a good meal.

The first Thanksgiving came to the Europeans by invitation from Native Americans who supplied most of the food. Back in the 1600's a young Indian by the name of Squanto wanted to have peace with the new people who had arrived here, so he invited them to a big feast his people had to thank the Creator for a good harvest. This is where the Europeans learned about all the vegetables that were edible and the practice continued by the Europeans until Squanto's death. After that the Indians were never invited again.

Now days many people have forgotten the true meaning of Thanksgiving. To most it is just a day to have a big meal and then watch a ball game on television. We need to get back to the true meaning. The only reason the Indians had this big feast was to celebrate and honor the Creator for giving them a bountiful harvest. I sometimes wonder if the people living here today realize just how much God has blessed them. American soldiers give us freedom, but that's just a drop in the bucket as to what God has given us.

Be thankful for what you have this Thanksgiving because you may have less next year. Our government has left us up the creek without a paddle, so we had better learn to swim because the next thing they take will be our boats.

Jim Rose Watermelons

Born in the early 1930's in a small community known as Coxey, times were considered hard because we had the distinct honor of being called 'po folks.' Electricity had not yet come to our neck of the woods. We used coal oil for lighting our homes, a wood stove for cooking our meals and Highway 72 was still a dirt and gravel road.

My family consisted of my parents, Annie and Alburn Casteel, a sister Marion, a brother Jimmy and me. Dad bought two acres of land from my Uncle Jim and Aunt Flora Rose. The property had an old house on it where we lived for a time. Aunt Flora was my dad's sister and we then lived next door to them.

Uncle Jim Rose grew some of the best watermelons in this part of the country and was well known for it. He saved seeds every year to plant the next year and always planted them on the first day of May before the sun came up, never varying from this custom. Rumor had it that he brought the seeds back from Texas years before when visiting some kinfolk though I never knew for sure. If anyone wanted to plant this kind of melon, they had to get the seeds from Uncle Jim and they soon became known as the Jim Rose Watermelon.

Uncle Jim always planted a large patch of them. Jimmy and I were still very young when one day we thought that his watermelons might be ripe; so we slipped over to his patch. We thumped the melons with our finger but could not tell if they were ripe so we used our knives to cut small squares in the melons and lift them out to see if they were red on the inside. If not, we put the plug back in the melon.

We happened to look up to see Uncle Jim coming our way from his house. We ran to a field with tall sage grass in it to hide from him, but Uncle Jim, with his bird dog nose, walked right up on us. He marched us back home and told mom what we had done where we received a lesson as to why we should not do that again. Mom applied the lesson with a peach tree limb.

That was the only whipping I ever received for slipping into Uncle Jim's watermelon patch, but not the only time I did it. We just became a little wiser. It was a yearly thing to visit the patch. Even as teenagers there was nothing quite as good as one of his melons when the dew had fallen and cooled them off.

We may have thought we were pulling something over on him, but he was a wise old bird. He always knew we were getting into his melon patch and I believe he got joy out of us thinking we were pulling something over on him.

Uncle Jim and Aunt Flora and their family were people loved very much and it was a joy to live next door to them. Uncle Jim was a devout churchgoer, so I liked to believe he is planting his melon seeds up in heaven and have to believe that the Good Lord is now slipping into Uncle Jim's watermelon patch. I wonder if He knows they are better after the dew falls on them. What am I saying? He knows everything.

Sometimes You Get What You Deserve

In our country, some years ago the majority of people believed in God and most seemed to be very happy but now most everyone thinks we are in terrible shape here. It seems the majority has turned away from God and that is a real shame. God created something so beautiful and unbelievable for us to live on; it is hard for people to comprehend what all He did for us.

It seems to me that God is very angry at the people in America and all over the world today. It doesn't take a genius to understand this, but there are some highly educated folks who may not believe it. It seems to me that God is angry at the way His creation is being treated and destroyed. He is angry at filthy television programs; angry at the greed, the murders, theft, cursing and the bad mouthing of others. For all these reasons America is probably getting just what it deserves.

It's only human nature for most to want the best of everything they can get; the best house, car, job and the most money. A greedy person has a better chance of getting those things because he is willing to break all the rules to get them. It seems to me that greed has become like a religion and it amazes me that people give up happiness and contentment just to have more.

Our government has worked hard to get rid of God completely in our lives. They have just about sold us down the drain. Do you ever wonder why we are so far in debt when the working people pay about half of their earnings for taxes? Did you ever think we would have to borrow money from China to keep our country running? It blows my mind that the government spends all the tax money they collect. Yes, there is something very wrong in Washington. God isn't only angry at the people but also our government.

Thanksgiving Day used to be a day to relax, enjoy a good meal with family and give thanks and praise to the Creator for all He blesses us with, but now it looks like it is a day to line up at shopping malls for Black Friday. Some stores even open on Thanksgiving Day. Maybe they need to change it from Thanksgiving Day to Black Friday Eve. Black Friday appears to be a day for people to go crazy and I wonder how God sees it.

There are many bad things happening here today; hurricanes, tornadoes, earthquakes, fires and other destructive events. People don't understand why and blame it on Mother Nature or global warming and they may be right; but who controls Mother Nature? God Almighty does. Could it be that He is trying to warn us that things are not right according to His will? This world is in a mess and there is only one simple solution; the Creator who created it. What He is waiting for is the majority of people to ask. Maybe you'd rather wait for the government to straighten things out.

Alabama the Beautiful

Alabama the Beautiful—at least that is what the welcome signs read coming into our state. First impressions come from the first thing people see and the first thing they see entering our state is all the garbage and junk along the roadsides.

Limestone County is at the top of the list when it comes to trash along its highways. It makes me sick to so see all the mess along Highway 72 and I hate to think about what tourists might conclude from our roadsides.

We have litter laws to prevent this but does anyone ever get a ticket and pay the $500 fine? Once a highway patrolman told me that it did no good to write tickets for littering as the judges throw them out.

Many others in Limestone County feel as I do but maybe we need to demand that something be done about the problem. Our rivers and streams are in even worse shape than our highways. Since the Tennessee Valley Authority controls our waterways it should be their responsibility to get them cleaned up; we sure pay enough for our electricity.

There are some who put their garbage into plastic bags, toss them in the back of their pickups and drive fast enough for them to blow out onto the roads. There should be a law to require pickup truck owners to have a net over anything with the possibility of blowing out of the truck bed.

Traveling in many other states, I have yet to find one with roadsides as bad as ours. People don't realize how much God has blessed Alabama with. We have beautiful rolling hills, valleys and mountains along with many great rivers and streams, but now they are just about polluted beyond use.

It's a shame and I hate for visitors to come as they draw their own conclusions about the kind of people who live here

If the majority is satisfied with the litter along our highways and roads and the garbage in our rivers and streams, then maybe it's okay with you but there is few of us that are sick of the mess and want it cleaned up.

If you don't love Alabama and don't want to see it free of litter and our rivers free of garbage once again, then maybe we need to change the welcome sign to read, *Welcome to Alabama, the Beautiful Garbage Dump.* Better yet, just give it back to the ones it was stolen from years ago, the Native American Indians.

Greed

Years ago we could buy a good product for a decent price and most everything sold in stores was made in America. We could do an honest day's work for a fair wage. Neighbors were always ready and willing to lend a helping hand to anyone in need. No one had to lock their doors because there was no threat of robbery and God was welcome in the schools across America; the Ten Commandments hung on the walls of many buildings.

After some years, things started to change. People became more educated and expected to earn more money, which was only right. Prices of everything rose. When cold drinks went from five cents to six, I thought it was awful. When people earned more money, the government collected more taxes but for some reason though they needed to spend every penny of it.

Greed began to become a big problem here. *Webster's Dictionary* defines greed as "selfish desire to acquire more than one needs or deserves." The Bible says in Ephesians 4:19 that ". . . who, being past feeling, have given themselves over to lewdness, to work all uncleanness with greediness."

Greed begins at the highest political offices in Washington and trickles down to the richest of poor people. Ever wonder why a politician spends millions to get elected to an office that pays two hundred thousand? Greed is the reason we are trillions of dollars in debt and until we elect some honest people it will never get any better. But then again, it is hard for an honest person to get elected because people seem hooked on lying politicians.

Many factories here have moved their plants to foreign countries for the cheap labor to make their products, then ship them back here and sell them for a price as if they were made here, making a huge profit. Some say this is good business but I say its greed; but there again, our government does have something to do with their moving because corporate taxes are higher here in America than elsewhere.

Unemployment is the highest in years because of greed. Ever wonder why gas prices are going up? They would like for us to think it's because of all the trouble in the Middle East but I say it's because of greedy oil companies out to make millions in profit at our expense.

For years the middle class has been the ones who have paid the taxes to keep our country running; not the rich nor the poor, but the middle class. But now they are a dying breed. It will soon be only rich or poor and then Mr. Government, where will the tax money come from?

Will things get better in America? Can you change a greedy person into an honest person? It would take a miracle but after all is said and done, I think back to what the wise old Indians had to say about greed, "Because of greed, the white race will destroy themselves."

Love Is the Answer

We need to get back to living in a way that would please our God. It's hard to believe He is very pleased with the way many people act in our country today. We have got to go back to the beginning of time and realize we all came from love, because God is love. All people are related, even to wild animals and all living things, because we all came from the same Mother Earth. Before another race came to this country, Indians lived this way treating all things with the belief that they were related to all living things. Their lifestyle didn't do anything to go against Mother Nature.

Now we are at the point where many don't love or respect each other. There is so much greed, jealousy, racism, hate and injustice in our country it's a wonder that God still lets it stand. If people would only change the bad things in their hearts into love, just think how much God would bless this country once again—only love for one another will save mankind.

It is very easy when we get angry to strike out at someone, but it is very hard to love someone who hurts us. The lack of love for each other is what's hurts the people, the country, our society and our nation. That's the root of wars and diseases. It will take love to stop wars; love is the medicine for all our ailments. With that kind of love we could cure all the wrongs done to our Mother Earth.

When Jesus lived on the earth in His flesh body, He went out into the wilderness, fasted forty days and forty nights and then had His vision. It seems that only the Indian culture still believes in visions. Americans today think you are an idiot if you mention anything about having a vision but I'm sure Jesus would be very pleased if people would fast for days and seek a vision to live a better way of life with love in their hearts.

My God is a simple being who loves all people very much. It is my belief that He spends a lot of time praying for people here on His earth, even though He sees so many wrongs; He has not given up on us yet. It pains me to think of my God being very hurt for the way some treat His creation. He isn't looking to see what color our skin is: He is not looking to see if we are poor or rich. He does look to see what's in our heart. My God doesn't walk around with a cell phone to His ear looking for a computer because I don't believe those things will be in heaven. *I sure hope not*!

When the non-Indian goes into his church he prays for himself and others and for things to get better. When the Indian goes into his lodge or teepee he talks to God and thanks Him for all He has blessed him with. The non-Indian thinks with his mind: the Indian thinks with his heart. The Indian people want to be friends with the non-Indians: most of them hold no hard feelings about what happened, but non-Indians seem to have a hard time accepting them as friends. Indian people find it very easy to forgive but the ones that need to ask for forgiveness find it very hard to do. It is my prayer that God will find it easier to forgive.

There is only one thing that can solve all the problems between all people and that is love. Why is it that something so simple is so hard to do? If each of us could just forgive all those we think have done us wrong and learn to love them, just think how much better off we would be. It does not hurt the ones we hate; it only hurts us.

We must go back to doing some things the old fashioned way. Don't let us get caught up in the modern high tech world with the drugs, filthy movies, killings and bad language. God is a simple being and we the people should never forget that; so keep some things simple and God will be pleased.

Many Things Are Unbelievable

It is beyond my wildest imagination why in our country we now have to be careful where we speak about our Lord or display anything about God the Creator. We have become a nation that lets the government cram anything they want to down our throats. Have you noticed how hard they are working to take God out of our lives completely? In our schools we can talk and discuss any kind of religion except the one our country was founded on. It seems to me that if a student in school today stood up and said Jesus Christ is my Savior, they would be expelled.

The only time our government stands up is when a person of God says anything about a lowlife that does everything against what God teaches, and the good people stand by and let it happen. Do churches try to do anything about what is happening in our country? Don't people think that God might want them to stand up for Him sometimes?

This is the very reason it is sometimes hard for me to follow the religious ways of non-Indians. We have so many different religions and different views about the word of God—it is very confusing. It is so much easier to follow the spiritual ways of the Native Americans because it is so simple—just go by the rules that God laid down. We can pray anytime and anywhere we want to and no government official is going to tell us what we can or can't do about our spiritual ways. By the way, all the Indian schools teach about God the Creator and Jesus Christ the Savior.

Many churches ask their members to pray for the leaders in Washington. Why in the world would we want to pray for someone going against everything God stands for? This country is far from being the good old US of A anymore and I do pray for the leaders; that every one of them will get defeated in the next election. It is my prayer that we elect someone who will stand up for God the Creator.

Another thing beyond my imagination is how bad television has become. Many years ago it was a good source of entertainment. Now days it is a tool to teach people how to kill, murder, rape and every other lowlife thing you can learn about, but still more people watch television because they are hooked on this demoralizing machine and church going people are not immune to this contraption—especially soap operas.

Even news on television is now all bad. There are killings and robberies every day all over the country. Newscasters seem to thrive on bad news because we never hear any good. This is America, but it is becoming like a third world country—a killing field. There are many reasons for this; drugs are one. Our government is another, but the main reason is that people have turned away from God. It is unbelievable that so many now go astray, but if we look at the influential things in our modern world, it's not hard to understand.

The greatest learning objects in this country are no longer teachers or the preachers because they have been replaced by television, computers, internet and those little boxes we carry around in our hand. Still we wonder what went wrong and why so many bad things happen in our world today.

We Are Losing the Good Life

How in God's name did we have ever let things get in such a mess in what was once a good country? Have most of the people given up on God the Creator? Have we lost all sense of decency? Have all our morals just flown out the window? Whatever happened to respect? Have we become a nation that loves money so much that we would give up the opportunity to spend eternity in that wonderful place known as heaven?

Why in the world did we ever get in debt to China, a country we fought in Korea? Why do we send money to over a hundred and fifty other countries each year? Just give away billions of dollars? Why do politicians think they have to lie to get elected? If they are as bad as their opponents claim, they all need to be in jail.

Our leaders today seem to be doing away with the teachings of our Lord. They are good at passing laws going against what the Bible teaches. Many preachers say we need to pray for our leaders in Washington; but to me we need to be pray to the Creator to get rid of all those in office and get some people in there who love God and this country.

If people could only see the beauty and many gifts the Creator has provided for us to enjoy here on this earth, just maybe they would not be so ready to destroy them. But a greedy person is blind to the natural beauty of things; all he sees is a way to make money.

Born in 1932, I have seen bad times and hard times and know how it was to have to work to help make a living, but I have enough common sense to know that hard times will one day come again. What many people don't understand is that we live in a fast changing world with many problems and threats from other countries.

The Great Depression hit the country in the late 1920's. Could people today stand a situation like that again? It took many hard working and hungry people to do it but they knew that with God's help they could and they did.

Greed is one of our biggest enemies and one of the reasons for the Great Depression. It runs rampant today more than ever.

It seems to me that our government today is seen as a big joke by many other countries. They no longer respect us; they just use us for our money. Our God loving nation has been turned into a greed infested race track.

Greedy people have raped Mother Earth of most her raw materials leaving little for future generations. Can we ever get back to a good and decent lifestyle? It could happen but only with the help of the Creator. He is the only way we can do it, but first it looks like He will have to bring everyone to their knees before it happens. It would save a lot of heartaches and pain if we would just get on our knees right now and talk to the Creator.

Are You Satisfied

Are you someone who is satisfied with all the bad things happening in our country today, such as tornadoes, earthquakes, hurricanes, snow storms, fires and other destructive things that come around too often? If you are, just sit back, do nothing and they will get worse. If you would like things to get better, maybe you need to get on speaking terms with the Creator of this earth, because He is the only one that can solve the problems we now have.

People in our country have destroyed and desecrated the earth for years just to make money; Earth is sacred ground whether you believe it or not. Why would anyone want to destroy something so beautiful that God made with His own hands? Just for the love of money! It's easy to understand why God would be so angry at some people and allow bad things to happen here.

Most say it is just Mother Nature making the weather change and there is nothing we can do about it. They are so right. We can't. But who in the world do you think controls Mother Nature? You may think God is not that mighty but if you do, you serve a different god because the one I serve can do anything. You have just got to love Him enough and the more you do His will, the more He will bless you.

Sooner or later God will bring everyone to their knees. It seems to me that He is very angry for the way most people have treated His creation so the sooner you get down on your knees and let Him know that you are going to treat the earth with a lot more respect and do your part to help clean it up, the sooner we will see things improve.

Weather people and scientists tell us that the bad weather is normal because of Global Warming; that it is because of man and his destruction of everything in his path. Greed has taken over many people's hearts and their love for money has caused them to do anything to get it. Clear cutting forests lands was wrong—we should always leave some for future generations. The only ones to protest clear cutting were the American Indians.

The majority in this country doesn't even realize or care how important trees are to their livelihood but the money hungry timber people keep on cutting our trees and tornadoes will blow the remainder down. What do you think will happen to people when all the trees are gone?

Every time I travel Highway 72, it makes me heartsick and angry because of the garbage along the sides of the road. God sees every piece of junk and He also knows who is responsible for it being there. I'm not saying He caused the tornadoes to hit there, but after the cleanup is completed, if I lived along the highway, I would do everything possible to make sure it stayed clean.

People, there is only one solution to all the problems we have here and that is to get back to doing the will of God. Don't tell me that what is happening in our country is normal because I am old enough to know better. When I grew up, we never heard of a tornado. We never had to worry about bad weather; but that was before greed, bad attitudes, jealousy, locked doors, filthy television and a lot of other things went against God's will.

Have you ever thought that God may be trying to warn us with these things happening today? We have got to get back to putting God at the head of our table.

We Need to Go Back

There was a time in our great country when most people were trustworthy and friendly to one another. If one bought or sold something, a handshake sealed the deal; no paperwork was needed. It was simply a matter of trust but that was back when folks asked a fair price for what they sold and the buyers got a good product for their money.

Maybe if we went back to trusting one another again, asked a fair price for what we sold and loved and trusted our friends and neighbors, the goodness in our hearts might begin to take over and spread.

We need to go back to doing some things the old fashioned way. It would not only please us, but the Lord. It seems we are just not headed in the right direction any longer.

There is a movement today headed up by the devil. He works very hard to turn us against God and it seems to me he gains ground every day. Of his many weapons, television and the internet have just about fallen completely into his hands.

While I don't have answers to all our problems, God the Creator does. If we don't get back to doing His will, things will only get worse. As a youngster, we never heard of tornadoes and most of the thunderstorms didn't have the strong winds like today.

Back then, most people tried to do the right things and even if they didn't attend church, they still tried to do right. God blessed this country greatly for that and that is why I believe we need to go back to some of the old fashioned ways.

Most people watch television programs today that are nothing but junk. If our mothers or grandmothers sat there and watched them with us, would we still watch them? If not then maybe we shouldn't watch them either.

Things can be better but only with the help of God. We don't need to be in church every time the doors are open but we just need to get back to doing things that are right. Talk to the Great Spirit and listen to what He lays on your heart. He is always there waiting to help, if our hearts are ready to listen.

Many don't think God can speak to us because they listen only with their ears. But God doesn't speak through our ears; He speaks to our hearts and if your heart is cold, you will never hear Him.

Changing things in this country is so simple that most overlook it. If people could just have a change of heart and turn in the direction that pleases God, then He might bless us once again. God loved the old fashioned way, I believe. We've got to go back.

The Root of All Evil

Money is good if used right. It is necessary to get by in our world; without it we couldn't buy food because hardly anyone still raises a garden in our modern world. It seems there are two kinds of people in our country—the wealthy and the poor. The love of money is wrong and like the Good Lord said, "It is the root of all evil."

Craving money is destroying the American way of life. So many celebrities, drug dealers, politicians and others make millions of dollars every year; they make the big bucks, but those who fight for our freedom put their lives on the line in harm's way to keep the big money makers safe and rich. By the way, soldier's earnings are at the bottom of the pay scale.

Our country is filled with those who sometimes must choose between food and the medicine doctors so freely put them on. For sure this isn't the America I grew up in.

If we all worshipped money like many do, it seems to me that God would have already destroyed the earth. Just think what a wonderful place to live it would be if everyone loved each other like they do their money.

Look at all the damage done to Mother Earth. It can be traced back to the love of money. If everyone loved God's creation like the American Indians do, He would still bless us greatly but the newcomers to our country didn't learn a thing from those who knew how to take care of it.

God didn't say that money was the root of all evil. He said, "The *love* of money is the root of *all* evil." So everyone and everything evil in this country can be traced back to the love of money. There are those who will do anything for money; rob, steal, cheat, lie and kill. They will do this to anyone. Many parents have been killed by their own children for the love of money.

There is nothing wrong with making lots of money; it's how you choose to use it that is the problem. There are rich who use their money according to God's will and they will be greatly blessed.

Why would anyone give up the chance to go to that wonderful place called heaven just for money? The time spent on earth is just a flicker of time compared to the time we will spend somewhere else and there won't be a need for money at either place.

People who turn away from God, turn away for the love of money. It doesn't matter how much wealth you possess, you cannot buy your way into heaven. Many play the lottery hoping to win a fortune, but few do. If I ever play, it's for one reason and that is to help the poor on the Indian reservations out west.

If I am worthy enough to make it to the place called heaven, no matter who meets me, Saint Peter or Jesus Christ, for sure my pockets will be empty.

Junk Mail and Waste

Have you ever wondered how many pounds of junk mail come through the Post Office each and every day? And how many trees it takes for just one day's delivery of this mail? The Post Office says it can't survive without the junk mail; it seems to me it would be safe to say that seventy-five percent of it goes from the mail box to the trash can without even being opened and looked at and seventy-five percent of the people don't recycle it either. What a shame to waste all of those trees.

Much of this junk mail comes from medical doctors trying to sell herbs. That alone should send up a red flag as I've never heard of a medical doctor going to school to study herbs. This appears to me as a rip-off for them to make more money. If you are going to take herbs you need to get them from a trained herbalist or an Indian medicine man or medicine woman.

First class mail at this moment costs forty-nine cents for a regular sized letter; in junk mail about twelve cents. People sending first class mail are usually paying bills or writing a letter to someone. On the other hand, people sending out junk mail do it to make money. The way I see it, if you are paying bills it costs you more, but if you send out junk mail to make money it costs you less. That's the way it goes in America; the people making the big money get all the breaks.

If we could send the junk mail back C.O.D. at junk mail rates, they would still pay less than first class mail. If the Post Office did this, they could almost double their money on junk mail, solve a lot of problems and save many trees. Here's another thought—just turn first class mail into junk mail. It would never get lost and be cheaper for people paying their bills—on the other hand, change junk mail into first class mail. This way a lot of it would get lost and many wouldn't send out so much and we could save many of our trees.

Why it is so hard for people to realize that we need to be saving our natural resources? Junk mail would not be so bad if everyone recycled it, but that is not yet happening because it is so much easier to do the wrong things; toss it in the garbage can or on the roadside.

A day will come when people will realize that all the waste they have created through the years will someday come back to haunt them. The time is coming when there will be shortages of items needed just to survive.

For this country's sake, please recycle everything you possibly can. We have been a wasteful nation for too long and the time has come for people to change their ways. Do you ever notice how much food is wasted in this country every day? Do you ever think about the Indian children on the reservations that go hungry every day? Do you ever wonder how the Creator feels about things like that? I believe He is fed up with a lot of people's actions and ways.

What we can save today will provide more for our children and grandchildren in the future and that is something that should concern us.

A Shame and a Disgrace

All the mess we've heard on the television about veterans and soldiers not getting the medical treatment they need by some hospitals and doctors is a shame and a disgrace to our country. If a veteran or soldier goes to a hospital for help and if service is not rendered immediately and they are put on a waiting list, then that hospital or doctor should be considered an enemy of our country!

If people in America can't respect our veterans and understand that if not for them, there would be no freedom. If we cannot accept this, maybe we just need to buy ourselves a ticket and get out of the country.

Some money hungry morons do everything and anything for money while our soldiers fight and die in other countries for idiots like them, and they have the gall to put a soldier or veteran on a long waiting list when they need help now, and all the while you do it for the money. You are no better than the enemy he is fighting against in other countries.

It might have come to the point that it's time to bring all our troops home to fight the enemy we have right here in our own country and that means going all the way to Washington D. C. if the need is there.

Our government is downsizing our military. Big mistake! They are only inviting other countries to invade us. A strong military will cause others to think twice before coming to or attacking our shores. It appears our government does not understand this. Another thing our government needs to learn is to keep their noses out of every little thing that happens in the world.

But what do I know about anything. This old veteran only has a little common sense. You know it took a lot of highly educated people with book sense minds to get this country into the shape it is today. Lord help us if they get any smarter.

For a long time I've said that education is not the answer to the problems we have, but our government keeps saying education is the answer. Just look at our highly educated government. If you think education is the answer, then I rest my case.

The answer to all our problems is to just get back to doing the things that are right. God gave us ten rules to live by—get back to living by them and our problems will go away. If the government lays down rules that go against God's rules, just ignore them; we will never go wrong going by God's rules.

All people need to thank the Creator every day for His creation and we need to thank veterans and soldiers every day for giving us the freedom to live in this great country.

There may be one other thing you need to do for God to bless us—make amends to the Native American Indians. I believe God is waiting for that to happen. No matter what rules the governments hands down, just remember to pray and talk to God anytime and anywhere you want to. It's not the government that will save us—only the Creator can do that.

Washington Needs a Front Porch

When they built Washington D. C., they made one huge mistake—they failed to build a front porch at the Senate and the House of Representatives buildings and to fill it with straight back chairs.

When I grew up most people were honest and trustworthy, and many important decisions were made on the front porch. Because there were no air conditioners it was hot inside the house, so the front porch was the coolest place.

This is where everyone sat late into the evening and planned out the next day's activities. We kids got our instructions for what we had to do the next day and it's where we received our punishment for something we had done that we shouldn't have.

The front porch served as a barber shop on the weekends where my dad cut hair. It is the place where we broke beans, shelled peas and shucked corn for canning for food during the coming winter months. The front porch is where we kids sat on Sunday evenings to watch for a car that might go by.

Any and all kinds of business that came up was probably settled on the front porch and most of the buying and selling also took place there. All that was needed to seal the deal was a handshake.

This all happened many years ago and we didn't need contracts or lawyers; just honesty. Maybe that's what we need in Washington so our Congressmen can get out of their fancy air conditioned offices and use the straight back chairs on the front porch. Maybe if they sweat a little and get their blood pumping in their body, they just might want to work a little.

But since they don't have a front porch, just take off those fancy suits, put a tee shirt and blue jeans on and get out under a shade tree on the White House lawn and go to work. They don't need chairs. Just sit on the ground and get close to nature, something they know nothing about. Let the ants get a taste of them and if a dog comes along and heists his leg and pees on one of them, don't worry about it. He just thinks they are an old, rusty fire hydrant. Besides they need to get a little taste of nature.

Just maybe the trees they sit under will be full of birds and all of them will get the urge to go to the restroom at the same time. Would they know what was going on or would they think, "We are getting an early snowfall." A little fertilizer on top of the brain might do some of them a world of good.

Many people in this country deserve a lot better than what we have in Washington today. There are some that don't even deserve what we do have. There is a new epidemic spreading across the country like wildfire. It is FUWOG, meaning Fed Up With Our Government. Sometimes it only makes sense to make changes and sometimes it's just time to flush the commode and get rid of some of the old _____.

God Bless America Again

God Bless America Again has been spoken by and prayed for by many preachers. Many songs have been written with this phrase in them but before we pray this prayer, maybe we need to realize what God expects from us. Most of us believe that God created the earth and with this in mind can we see why He might not want to bless our country again?

If you cannot understand that; then look at the roadsides in North Alabama. Is all this garbage appealing to God, the Creator? Every piece of trash desecrates His creation and the shape our rivers, creeks and streams are in must bring tears to His eyes.

Turn your television on and within five minutes you will see other reasons why He may not want to bless America, not to mention the internet and the filth that can be found there.

There are many reasons God may not want to bless our country. Just look to our government; about everything they do goes against His will. They have taken prayer out of schools and children are killing children. We cannot display the Ten Commandments in government buildings and they legalized the killing of unborn babies. How do you think God feels about this?

The newscasts on television are about people robbing and killing others. Greed has taken over many hearts. How in the world can we expect God to bless a country like ours?

When the first white Europeans came to this country killing Indians, taking their homelands and claiming that God had willed them this land, it was all right. The Indians were God's people and the only race that treated the earth with the respect God expects. It seems to me that God is very angry at them for doing that and is still angry at people and government for putting His people on reservations and treating them like they are not even human.

God is not going to bless America if He is very angry at the people. He has tried to warn everyone that things are not right; tornadoes, earthquakes, fires, hurricanes and many other bad things keep happening. We never had to worry about these kinds of things when I was young. Is this a warning from God? It is, but you may not believe it.

91

If we want God to bless America again, the first thing we need to do is make amends to the Indian people. These people are our brothers and sisters if we are true believers in God, treat them like family. Everyone needs to work to clean up our highways and waterways. Our litter laws need to be enforced, maybe even double the fines. The Tennessee Valley Authority controls the rivers so they should have the responsibility for cleaning them up.

If we don't get back to doing the things that are right, treating Mother Earth as sacred ground, working to get greed out of our hearts and not knowing the secrets of having a better life, then we should ask the Indians. Most of them will give us seven words to live by: Honesty, Knowledge, Wisdom, Respect, Love, Humility and Bravery or Courage. Maybe someday we will get back to the point where God will bless America again.

Amish Christmas

In 2001 I decided to build a log house down on the Elk River. The company that sold me the logs suggested a crew of Amish people they had used. David Gingrich was in charge of the crew and they agreed to build my house.

During the time they built my house, David and his crew became friends of mine. Since then our friendship has grown and includes David's wife Mary. They only had two children at the time, Josh and Mariah but now have three more children living; Judith, Diane and Kari.

We have visited each other's homes many times and their family is very dear to me. I love them very much. Mary is a very good cook and on occasion during my visits she baked bread or cookies, always sending some home with me.

David called me about a week before Christmas to invite me to come to their school to see their children do a little Christmas presentation. I gladly accepted, and the Thursday evening before Christmas drove to the school, between Summertown and Hohenwald, Tennessee. Arriving a little early I took a seat at the back of the room; the girls were practicing one of their songs. David and Mary's little girl

Diane saw me and waved, then looked around at the other girls like she Might have done the wrong thing.

There were about twenty five students in the school from first grade up whom all had parts. Each one did their part without missing a word and knew the words to all the songs. It amazed me that the young children learned and remembered all of their parts.

It was a joy to be among them and to listen to the children give praise and honor to God and Jesus Christ. It was just pure and simple worship of our Savior. Not influenced by the outside world, they focused on giving our Lord the praise He deserves.

The girls were dressed in full length dark maroon dresses with prayer caps on their heads. The boys were dressed in dark pants, white shirts and wore suspenders. They all looked very nice. After the program, they didn't run out to get a cell phone stuck in their ear. They did not have to worry about getting home to get in front of a television or to get on a computer to play video games. My guess is that when they returned home, they put their night clothes on and laid down knowing that they had done the Lord's will that night.

The sole purpose of their Christmas program was to celebrate the birth of Jesus Christ and the children did a wonderful job of that. It was truly a blessing for me to be a witness to the occasion.

Outsiders who live in a fast paced, high tech world don't seem to impress the Amish at all. It sure doesn't impress me anymore. The Amish live a good life because they put their Creator first in their lives, just as Native American Indians did before intruders landed on our shores.

Many Lies Written

History books written and used when I was in school told many lies about my Indian ancestors, calling them names such as savages, heathens and other derogatory names. The writers of those books knew they were lies and they would be used for children to study and learn what they thought was the truth about Indian people. These writers got paid to cover up the real truth and make the government look good for killing Indians.

During the Indian Wars, writers did everything within their power to make the Indians look bad and the white men and governments look good. When the Indians began the Ghost Dance, it was to bring the buffalo back and to raise their dead ancestors. It was a dance with hope for the future but the writers wired information back to newspapers in the East that all hell was about to break loose and those murdering redskins were going to kill everyone.

The information they sent was nothing but lies. They knew that, but it made a good story for the readers who hated Indians. The lies they thought they had to write caused many Indians; men, women and children, to be slaughtered. All that killing was just another good story for their readers but to me they were very low-life human beings.

Those writers thought they could write anything against the Indians and the Europeans would believe it—and they did, because they hated Indians. Many people are now finding out about all the lies written about the Indians but never considered that the Creator knew it all along. Will they feel like big men when they meet our Savior or will they beg for mercy?

If the Indian people could have written their side of the story during the Indian Wars it would have been much different than the white man's version. Indian's spiritual beliefs would not have let them lie; it would have only been true facts.

Many writers today still pick up on what earlier ones said about our early history and believe it to be the truth. So they keep passing down the same information from generation to generation. My own thoughts and doubts include knowing in my heart that the white men will write everything he can to make them look better than the Indians.

It is my belief that early writers during the Indian Wars were responsible for as many or more deaths than the military because of the lies they put into print and that many Indian men, women and children died because of them. That is a heavy burden to carry to meet the Creator.

Those who called themselves Christians and killed Indians and those writers who lied about them, if they knew anything about God the

Creator, they had to know they did wrong. But would our history be very different today if they had the opportunity to do it over?

My Friend Spencer Black

Most of us have many friends and some of them are special. One of my great and special friends was Spencer Black, someone who never met a stranger. He was the kind of person that if you had never met him before, once you did, you would for sure know him the next time the two of you met. Our friendship spanned many years; we rode to work together for some years and it was always a pleasure to be around him.

It is safe to say that Spencer did more for Limestone County than any other individual and most people would agree. Often when we rode around solving the world's problems, someone holding an office in Limestone County would call to get his opinion and suggestion on some problem that had come up. This happened many times but he never refused to give them an answer as to how he would handle it and most of the time they took his advice. He not only helped Limestone County but also helped Rogersville in Lauderdale County too. Not many people knew about all the many things and people that he helped.

Spencer had book learning, but what made him great was that he had a head full of common sense, too. We became very close when I moved back to Limestone County from Walker County. He seemed to think that at my age, someone needed to watch over me. If he didn't come by my home every two or three days, he called to check on me. He always called me Lone Elk. His words were, "I just called to see if you were still alive. I don't want the buzzards flying over your house with you laying up dead and no one knowing about it."

One thing we enjoyed was to visit the Amish people where we both had friends. My friend Herman Gingrich, who makes log furniture and sells vegetables, really liked Spencer who told him jokes when we were there. Finally Herman began to tell Spencer jokes and after that they tried to outdo each other. Herman still tells me, "I sure do miss old Spencer."

When the two of us were out together, we talked of different things and seemed to be on the same wave length about right and wrong. We had many conversations about Native American Indians and the wrongs they had to deal with for many years. He wanted to help and one day asked me, "How can we help these people?"

They were in need of most everything but I said the need for clothes, especially winter clothes, would be a great help. Spencer said, "You find out where we need to carry them. I can get a truck and enough clothes donated to fill it." That was our plan and Spencer was excited about it saying, "After I carry my family out West on vacation, we will do this."

If only Spencer could have lived to carry one load to the Pine Ridge Reservation in South Dakota and see how these people had to live, it would have touched his heart so much that it likely would have become his lifelong goal to help them. Spencer Black had a big heart and was beginning to feel the Indian blood in his body. There is no doubt about what he would have done.

Not only did Limestone County lose one of its great leaders, but the Indian people out West lost someone who would have been a great help to them. I knew Spencer as well as anyone outside his family did and knew in my heart that if he had ever set foot on one of those reservations, met some of the people and saw the conditions they had to live in; they would have had a friend for life.

My nephew Chris Casteel went with me to a Sun Dance in the Black Hills of South Dakota about the middle of June. It was unforgettable and the most spiritual event I have ever witnessed, but Spencer was what was missing. He would have met many friends among the Indian people and had he been alive he would have been there with us.

There are not enough words for me to express all the good feelings I had for this great person. His kind is what makes this country a better place. His popularity reached all the way to Montgomery, Alabama and it was a great honor for me to have Spencer Black as a friend. His family misses him very much. I loved him like a brother and hardly a day passes that I don't think about him but he is now in a better place, still watching over me. We talked a lot about that place called heaven.

96

What Will Happen Next?

We live in a world that is forever changing and now it is not changing for the best. Our government does things that please the devil but not the Creator. While there are still many good people, there are many more working for the devil.

Television has a hold on people so bad that they don't even believe there is a Creator. Many only call on the Lord when they are ready to draw their last breath, though it may be too late then.

It amazes me that others can't see where our country is headed when it is as plain as the nose on our face. Many people believe the bad weather and other bad things happen as a natural thing but it isn't natural at all. If they can't see that things get worse when we turn away from God, they probably can't see the nose on their faces.

From one day to the next we wonder what will happen. When we hear about something, it is usually bad and it is not good to live in a country where bad things happen almost every day. There are so many who don't care one way or the other and young people think this is a natural way of life.

God said all things are possible if we believe it strong enough. It is possible to have a good country once again if we believe it and do what God expects us to do. Does the Creator want us to live in the conditions we have today? God wants us to be happy and have good lives without having to deal with all the sicknesses and diseases we have.

What's happening now? Well there is a new television program called Dating Naked. It makes me wonder what is coming next and we can bet it will be worse. Our government is at each other's throats all the time and the only good thing about it is that maybe they won't have time to pass more stupid laws. Young people become highly educated in modern technical fields but without a machine can't tell the time of day. They can't add, subtract or multiply without a machine and their pleasure comes from machines also. Makes one wonder what will happen when the internet shuts down and it will happen one day.

What our young people need to learn is some common sense, sometimes called just plain old horse sense. They need to learn about nature, the names of the trees, about the animals and about God the

97

Creator and where life came from. Most kids today cannot tell you the difference between the call of a bullfrog and a hoot owl.

If we want God to bless our country again, we need to get rid of greed, hate, racism, bad tempers and let God know that we will do the things He expects of us. One of the first things most people need to do is make amends to the Indians. There has never been a race so mistreated and God is angry about it. Will you be one He will hold accountable?

Do you ever wonder why the native people in our country had no kind of disease? It was because God gave them good health and they looked to the Great Spirit for guidance in everything they did and never harmed His creation. Just look at our country today if you want to know why God is angry.

He hasn't given up on people yet but if He doesn't see some changes in the near future, it will all be over one day.

Where Is the Justice in America?

Sometimes justice is hard to come by or recognize. Many seek it but few find it. Most of those who worked in the twin towers when the horrible 911 attack happened probably earned $100,000 or more. They had good jobs and made good money and many likely had good savings accounts and large insurance policies.

On the other hand, there were many who had no jobs. Many were homeless and went through soup lines to get something to eat and many of them were veterans who had survived horrible war.

Our government is giving surviving families of the 911 attack from $250,000 up to $4.7 million with an average of $1,185,000. That's a pretty good paycheck for someone who already earned above average wages.

Now look at what the survivors of American soldiers who died fighting for our freedom get. The first check is a $6,000 direct death benefit, half of which is taxable. Next, they get $1,750 for burial costs. Surviving spouses get $833 a month until they remarry and there is a payment of $211 per month for each child under age eighteen, ending on their eighteenth birthday.

Surviving soldiers who fought in battle and remain in service for twenty years, retiring at E-7 level will receive a pension of $1,000 per month.

Now look at Congress, who vote themselves a pay raise any time they wanted to. They do not receive Social Security at retirement because they don't have to pay into the system. They only need to serve in Congress for one term to receive a pension of more than $15,000 monthly and most of them are millionaires when they leave office.

Still, some of our veterans without arms or legs live homeless on the streets selling pencils to get a dollar or two. Other veterans are about the only ones who help them. A soldier goes to war and fights for everyone's freedom and many die doing so. They do it for the love of country, surely not for the money because they are at the bottom end of the pay scale.

There are pro ball players and movie stars who make millions and all they do is supply us with a little entertainment. Apparently entertainment is more important to most people than their freedom. It makes one wonder what kind of entertainment we would have if not for the soldiers who died for our freedom.

Since the government has done such a great job of getting our country so far in debt we will never get out, now the president is going to take over the health insurance program. If we don't buy ourselves an insurance policy, we will have to pay a fine. Just look at the shape our country is in today; then we will know how our medical insurance will be. The poor working people will not be able to survive and that may be the government's intent.

The Young People of Today

Younger generations today have every opportunity in the world to be anything they choose or want to be. What they don't realize is that it has not always been this way and in years to come, opportunities may not be as good as now in our forever changing world.

When young, the only opportunity I had other than to go to school was to work in the fields to help our family make a living. The work was hard and dirty and regular; there were no telephones or cell phones in our homes; no radio or television. For a long time, we didn't even have electricity and for a time, Highway 72 was still a dirt and gravel road. Can you picture yourself living in a world like that?

What we did have back then that seems lacking today was happiness. God's creations were our playground and believe me; we took every opportunity we could to do the things we loved. We hunted in the woods, fished on the river and if we had a couple of free days, camped out on the riverbank. We didn't even know what the word bored meant.

We learned young about the different types of fish in the rivers and creeks and also the different kinds of trees—many of which supplied us with food. We knew about every tree, bush or vine that had edible food and could have lived off the land.

We seemed to have more fun and enjoy life to the fullest without the high-tech, fancy inventions we have today. Probably the reason so many are bored is because they have so much. Even with everything they could ever want yet, they don't seem to have anything that makes them happy. Are they looking for happiness in the wrong places? Anyone who thinks drugs are the answer to their happiness, is dead wrong. The only things drugs will bring are heartache, misery and a plot in the cemetery.

What our young people today don't realize is that all the things they have today are because of the freedom in this country. Do they even have a clue about who gives them this freedom? No, it is not the government. They have nothing to do with it. It is the soldiers who have fought and died for many years, just so we can live in a country with freedom and so much more. Just think for a minute—would one give their life so others could live?

When one decides to get into drugs and other wrong things, just think about the soldiers who died to make ours a better life. They sure didn't do it so we could do drugs and other bad things. The first thing we need to do is honor the Creator of this earth; honor our parents, elders and the soldiers and veterans. It might be surprising how much better one feels.

There are many good kids in America and they have a hard time resisting all the pressure they face every day. It is so important to stay strong and keep the faith.

Our government is leaving our youth with the biggest challenges this country has ever faced, so don't follow in their footsteps. They never seem to care about future generations.

To the young people who think drugs are the answer to their problems, just leave those who are trying to do the right things alone. They will be the leaders of this country some day and if you are not yet in the cemetery, you will probably be in a mental institution and need someone to lean on.

To continue to use drugs leaves only two options, but just remember; each of us has the opportunity to be someone great, but drugs were more appealing and the only ones to blame is yourselves. There is always help if you really want it. Just talk to God and He will show you the way.

Happiness – It Will Never Be Like It Was Before

We have come far since 1950 when I became employed by the United States Military. At that time, we seemed to be move along at a comfortable pace with a decent lifestyle but nowadays, many changes have come about and so many new things have been invented that make our lives much easier.

But it seems to have come too far too fast for people to enjoy all of the progress. We now live our lives in a fast-paced lifestyle with no hope of ever slowing down. Is this true happiness or have we lost the meaning of what that is all about?

My thoughts are that we have lost something we can never get back; like God gave us the opportunity to find happiness in our early years and many of us found it, but now many more cannot find the time

101

to look for it. People think it's just around the corner or at the next shopping center and cannot comprehend the meaning of what it is. Before we can find happiness, we have to have contentment in our hearts and that can't be found in such a fast-paced way of life.

God gave us two of the most important things in life to look for—love and happiness but if we miss out on these two things, misery will follow us the rest of our lives. If I had not found love and happiness in my life, the first thing I would have done is have a good long talk with God, the Creator. He has a road map to all things.

Don't go to shopping centers looking for happiness. That's where we are likely to meet Mr. Aggravation. We need to just spend some time alone, let our minds take a rest, let good thoughts flow into our hearts and we will feel contentment begin to take over our body and happiness will soon show up. It's not so hard. We just have to get in the right frame of mind.

We can't go back to the good old days, because of our government and the manufacturers of the little gadgets that we carry around in our hand and stand in line to purchase. We have lost the will to find happiness and found the will to take everything we can get our hands on and for that reason we are missing out on one of God's greatest gifts.

Happiness will never come to many because of their love for money. True happiness came to me at a very young age when I could walk down by the creek, sit and listen to the waters gently flowing downstream and hear nothing but the sounds of nature; birds singing and wild animals talking to each other. Just to look around and see all the things that the Creator has provided for our enjoyment makes a heart overflow with joy and happiness.

Today people rarely experience that because of all the high-tech noise and no one has the desire anymore which is just too bad because they will never know the joy of contentment. No, it will never be like it was before.

Just My Opinion

Things will ever be the same as they once were; not only time has changed but a lot of things we once held dear to our hearts have. Here are some things we need to bring back in my opinion.

All classes in every school in the United States need to begin the day with the Pledge of Allegiance to the Flag. Every school, state and federal office in our government need to have a copy of the Ten Commandments hanging on their walls, not just for show but for a guideline to go by when making any decision.

Prayer needs to be reinstated in all our schools. If there are some who have a different kind of religion with different beliefs, let them build their own schools. Every sports event in our schools needs to have prayer before the competition begins. Why would we not want to pray for the safety of our children?

No matter how smart and educated one becomes, no matter how many new inventions come along to make life easier, our Creator will always be the same as He was in the beginning. He gave us the knowledge to be and do most anything we want to do or be, but He did not limit them to be right or wrong. We choose the right path and He will bless us. We choose the wrong path and He will punish us.

True history needs to be taught in our schools. Students need to know this land was stolen from the Indians and that many were slaughtered in the process. They need to know how black people came to be in this country for the sole purpose of being slaves to big plantation owners.

Christopher Columbus, a person credited with discovering America and who has a day set aside on our calendar to honor him, never set foot on our country. He was a killer and a drunk along with being a liar that brought all kinds of diseases to the island he landed on. The Indians he killed along with the ones who died from the diseases, almost destroyed the population on the island.

Andrew Jackson became president because he loved to kill Indians and he was very good at it. William H. Harrison was elected president for the same reason. Years ago, history books did not tell the truth. There are so many more wrongs that true facts never came out about. Young people today need to know these things. Children are taught to tell the truth, so why do we teach them lies in school?

School children need to be taught where their freedom comes from. They need to know that hundreds of thousands of American soldiers gave their lives in battle for the freedoms we now have. Many of those soldiers were Indians and black people. When we see a veteran, we should thank him for the freedom we still enjoy.

Today young people seem to get their education by the usage of computers. Many learn a lot from television—big mistake. They may learn how to be a very smart person, but will they know how to be happy? Will they know how to hunt and fish? Will they know the different kinds of trees? Will they know all the different kinds of birds and animals? Will they know anything about nature? Will they know how to survive?

In my opinion it is very important to learn about the Creator. Without Him, there would be no earth or life upon it. When our government took God out of our schools, that's when many of our problems began. We never heard of killing in any schools before that.

Many people in this country think they know more than our Creator. In my opinion the young people today need to realize that these kinds of people are nothing more than walking idiots. If we will make God the Creator first and foremost in our lives, we will never go wrong. When we are down and out about something, please don't go to drugs for answers. Just go to God our Creator. He has the answers to all our problems.

If the people in this country want things to get better, there is only one solution—God the Creator. He can stop the bad weather, earthquakes and put out the fires. There is only one thing the majority of people have to do—go by His rules. These are just my opinions.

For God's sake, don't let the government send your soul to hell.

What Is Coming Next?

We all wonder what is going to happen next, living in some of the most troubling times in our history. If it is not the threat of terrorists, it is the threat of bad weather or earthquakes. While many wonder why we live in these conditions, many others think all of this is just normal.

One of the reasons for these conditions is because we are a nation that has drifted away from the rules handed down from the Creator. He has always been in charge of the earth, and always will be. When the majority steps away from His teachings, bad things are going to happen.

When God created the earth, it was to stand forever, and I believe it will. Ecclesiastes 1:4, "One generation passes away, and another generation comes: but the earth stands forever." Many are destroying this earth just as hard and fast as they can. The Creator had something to say about that. Revelation 11:18, "Time is rapidly approaching for God to bring to ruin those ruining the earth." Just think of the many people who are ruining this earth just for the love of money.

Here are some other quotes from God's word. Proverbs 22:28 "Do not remove the ancient landmark which your fathers have set." I believe this is a direct message to the European people who so freely destroy Indian mounds and burial sites of Native Americans.

Here is another quote, Proverbs 21:13, "Whoever shuts his ears to the cry of the poor will also cry himself and not be heard." Indian people have been crying for many years. Their young children go to bed hungry almost every night without enough cover to keep them warm. The U. S. Government, most people and most churches ignore them. I wonder how the Creator feels about this.

Being an older person and seeing all the changes that have taken place in this country, I can understand what and why there are so many destructive things going on in today's world. In simple terms God can send more destruction and hell to people doing wrong than we ever dreamed of, but still we wonder what's going on.

Can we ever get back to being a country that the Creator can look down on and smile and say, "Well done, my children?" Have we come too far to still believe there is a Creator? The more educated our country becomes it seems the further we get away from God's teachings and it makes one wonder if they are teaching the wrong things in our schools.

Time will tell if we are headed in the wrong direction from what the Creator expects of us. The problem with this is, if we do realize we are it might be too late to do anything about it. There are many who claim to be Christians, but do they truly believe what God says? My guess is that we could not find one in a million who believes they could move a mountain. Did God not say that if you have the faith and believe it strong enough that you can move a mountain? He just might be trying to tell that if we have the faith and believe it strong enough we could do a lot of things, maybe even cure ourselves from a lot of diseases, and calm the weather. We can have the power to do many things through God the Creator.

The Heaven I Dreamed

One night I dreamt of crossing over from this life to my new home above and upon arrival the Lord said, "Welcome Home, My son. I have been looking forward to your arrival. You have much to see. Come, let me show you around."

We went to a long hallway with many doors. He said, "I will let you look into a few." When we came to the first door, He said, "They are from the Baptist church." Inside were streets of gold and many mansions. People were dressed to a tee and the preacher was asking for more donations. The Lord said, "The Baptists try to out dress one another and the preacher has not yet learned that money is worthless here."

The next door was the Church of Christ and He said, "Now be real quiet when you look inside because they believe they are the only ones here."

The next door was the Methodists. He said, "They feel as they are the upper class and never want too many members in their church."

The following door was the Catholics and the Lord said, "Be careful when you look in as they can get a little wild." They were partying and drinking too much wine. The Lord added, "They know how to throw a party but tomorrow morning they will be in the Pope's office confessing."

"There are so many doors down this hallway," I spoke to the Lord. He said, "Yes, there are many new religions popping up every day with many different names on their buildings. A regular person could not keep up with them all."

Then He said, "You know, there are many different churches; some small, some large and fancy, but that's not what I see when I look at people. I look into their hearts."

Lord, I want to ask you something, "With all these heavenly places you have prepared for Your people, why are there streets of gold and bodies of water filled with litter and garbage?"

"You know son, we try to make them feel at home; that's the way they lived on earth and they liked it so much on My Creation and never offered to clean it up. But you don't have to worry about things like that anymore; Come, let's go see your new home."

We came to a door that read, *The First Native People*; we walked in to see the most beautiful place I've ever laid eyes on. The rivers and streams were crystal clear and filled with many different species of fish. Beautiful mountains, forest lands, valleys and prairies were filled with large herds of buffalo, wild animals and birds roaming and in the distance was the sound of beating drums.

"Lord, You knew the kind of heaven that would make us happy; the trails are not made of gold," I said.

The Lord said, "I would not insult Indian people by putting gold on their trails. They had too many problems with gold diggers on earth. Your people treated my Creation the way all people should have and for that, I made them a special place here."

"You were the only ones who used my Creation as your church. All your prayers I received; some came by eagle, some by smoke. Many times you looked up into my face, raised your arms toward heaven and prayed from your hearts directly to me. Every prayer was heard and you thanked me for the animals killed for food. No others have done that before and many will pay dearly for the way they treated your people.

"You will meet all your Indian brothers and sisters that paid the ultimate price on earth; they are all here. It will be a joy for you to listen to the great chiefs tell their stories while you sit around campfires at night. Chief Joseph, Sitting Bull, Geronimo, Red Cloud, Tecumseh, Quanah Parker and many more love to tell their stories. I spend a lot of time with my Indian people. They are very special to me. My son you are free to enjoy a life you have never known before and it will last forever more. Welcome home."

A Look through My Eyes

From my grandmother's words it is known to me that Europeans came into this country killing Indians and taking their land and claiming to be Christians; and that God told them it was the right thing to do. God, what can you do with idiots like that?

Always having been a good listener, in my younger years I realized I was better at listening than at talking. It blows me away with amazement at some of the things heard when in a crowd that loves to talk and blow their own horns. Sometimes I say to myself, "God did you hear that?"

What really amazes me is that many of the same people park their butts on a church bench every time the doors open and think they are the best Christians God ever put on the earth. Many have the answers to all the problems we have in this country and know how to fix them. One solution many have come up with is to get rid of those worthless Mexicans by running them back across the border or shooting them.

For some ungodly reason these European people think this is their country and always has been, but news flash—this is not their country; never has been and never will be. God owns this country and He gave it to the Indian people to have and to hold until the end of time. What they did to the native people when they killed and stole their land, makes me sometimes wonder if God can ever forgive them. They didn't even know they were killing their brothers and sisters in God's eyes and they want people to believe they are Christians?

What did the European government do to the Japanese people that were here when Japan bombed Pearl Harbor? Even though some had lived here all their lives, some were U. S. citizens, many were married to American citizens; but the government thought they needed to round all of them up and put them in filthy stockades—but still they think they are Christian people.

They brought ship loads of black people from Africa to be their slaves. They had already used Indians as slaves, and now they probably use Mexicans the same way. The big plantation owners liked to rape young Indian girls, young black girls and probably do the same to young Mexican girls—but still they are Christians.

European people think they are the superior race over all others—but they are superior over nothing. In fact, they may be on the bottom of the totem pole when it comes to the people God loves most. Still, they think they are the only Christians on the earth.

Why didn't they stand up against the blacks when they showed that they were not going anywhere? They could have killed them like they did the Indians and been Christians. Maybe the blacks had better weapons than the Indians and could not be slaughtered as easily as Indian women and children. In other words, they may have been cowards. Now does that make them less of a Christian?

It seems it doesn't take much in this country to be a good Christian. Just be ready to run all other races out of the country and own a good gun for killing people and yet, have the gall to criticize other people and their spiritual beliefs. I like to believe what Billy Graham had to say:

> "The greatest moments of Native history may lie
> ahead of us, if a great spiritual renewal and awakening
> should take place. The American Indian has been a
> sleeping giant. He is awakening."

Extra Special Friends

As we go down all the trails we will travel in our lifetimes, we will meet many people with different views and opinions about life. Many will share their feelings. Some we will soon forget but many will become friends and a few will become extra special friends. Some years back I met a family of this nature and it did not take me long to realize that how very much I loved them and felt their love for me. They are a family where love blossoms.

Sean and Yvette's family including her brother, Mark, do the things that are right, because they are as close to the Creator as anyone I know of. He is first and foremost in their lives along with their children. Their lives revolve around the Creator, their family, friends, animals and helping ones in need. They heard about how some of the original line of horses the Choctaw and Cherokee took with them on the Trail of Tears march out West were going to be put down so they went out West and brought back trailer truck loads of these animals to their farm in Lauderdale County, Alabama. They were not going to let those beautiful horses become extinct.

Sean and Yvette are the kind of people that will be glad to pray with you or for you. No one believes in prayer any more than they do, including Mark. How thankful I am they chose Alabama to move to from California.

Their farm is named *Sacred Way Spirit Horses and Buffalo Sanctuary*. They not only have wild horses but also five buffalo; Medicine is the name of the white bull and the brown females are known as Sweet Grass, Cedar, Blue Corn and Smoke, along with many other animals. I have never seen a couple so dedicated to their family, their animals and their spiritual way of life. Spiritual people of this caliber are hard to find today and any time I've been around them, the presence of the Lord is felt.

Sean and Yvette invited me to go to a Sundance in the Black Hills of South Dakota. My nephew, Chris Casteel, agreed to go with me and the trip was the most humbling and rewarding experience of my life, learning many things about the spiritual ways of Native American Indians. Now, I see why God loves these people so much. If you think you know everything about God and His ways, just go to a Sundance and

110

see how much can be learned. Dances at the Sundance is just another way of praying to the Creator and be assured that everything done there is to honor Him and His presence is always felt.

Yvette's Ancestry: Her mother's side is Cheyenne, Arapaho, Comanche and Mayan. Her father's side is Natoka, Choctaw or Cherokee. Sean is of the Cherokee and Euchee tribes. They travel all over the country and many foreign countries spreading the word about the spiritual ways of the Indian people; not only praying with but also helping them.

At the Sundance, Yvette and Mark danced every dance encouraging those outside the circle to join in, so I did. It amazed me at how much power was felt coming from dancers inside the circle. Another thing that amazed me was that Yvette was with child and each dance lasted from an hour to an hour and a half, four times a day for four days while fasting.

About three months after the Sundance, Yvette gave birth in a teepee on their farm to a baby boy. Later they called me and said they needed to talk to me. We met at Big Spring Park in Tuscumbia during the *Return to Coldwater* Festival. They had the baby with them along with Cruz and Huyanha. They said, "What we wanted to ask you is, 'If you will be the baby's godfather?'" After getting over the shock, I said, "Yes. It would be the greatest honor ever received." Then Yvette put the baby in my arms and said, "Nakota Braveheart, meet your godfather." She then said, "You are the first one to hold him outside of the family." My thoughts were Thank You, God. Thank You, God.

Knowing Yvette and Sean loved me still I never dreamed of something like this happening. They will never know the feelings inside me that day, and they will never know how much happiness they put in my heart to be the godfather of such a beautiful baby boy. It is beyond my greatest dream.

Sean and Yvette have my eternal gratitude for treating me like part of their family. I love this family very much and it is an honor to associate with people like them. If this country had more people like them, God would smile greatly on us once again

The Eagle

The eagle is the mightiest of all birds; large and powerful birds of prey with a powerful bill. Its broad and strong wings enable it to soar in flight not flapping its wings like other birds. It sits on a high ledge or tall tree and waits for the right wind current to take off and soar high into the sky with little effort.

Eagles mate and use the same nest for life. When a mate dies the survivor mourns a long time before searching for another one. They create their nests, up to ten feet wide, twenty feet deep and weighing over a ton, in safe places, often cliff ledges or tall tree tops. They are very kind and gentle parents, sharing the responsibility of caring for their young. The babies are ready to learn to fly after about three months. The mother thrashes around in the nest until one of them falls out and begins flapping its wings. The mother flies underneath the baby, catching it on her back and returning it safely back to the nest. This continues until each of them can fly.

Their eyesight is so good they can spot a rabbit or even a mouse from two miles away and can soar up to one hundred miles an hour. Their bones are hollow therefore they are light of frame.

Eagles have two spans in their lifetime. After about thirty years, they find a secret place and claw at their feathers and tear out damaged ones from their faces and other parts resulting in bleeding. This is necessary for the eagle to renew its strength and enable it to live another thirty years.

Long before white people landed on these shores, Native Indians believed the eagle to be a sacred bird. They believed the eagle carried their prayers to the Creator because it could fly higher than any other bird. It is ironic that Indians had these feelings for thousands of years and the Holy Bible mentions the eagle thirty eight times. Perhaps the Indians knew something the whites had not learned.

Like the buffalo, the eagle was near extinction at the hands of the same people. Killing animals and birds for the simple pleasure of it makes me wonder that they don't understand how all living things are related.

112

After years of the slaughtering of this great bird by Europeans, it became the iconic symbol of America. One would think that those who brought the Bible to this country, portraying themselves as Christians, would have had more respect for them since they are mentioned so frequently in the scriptures.

It would be wonderful to see eagles come back along the banks of the Elk River but it's not likely to happen because in the wild, they are such a clean bird. If they flew over the Elk River today and saw the garbage and junk along its banks, it's my belief they would fly on to a cleaner body of water.

The Sun Dance

There are many in this great country of America with different religions and beliefs. Most who practice their religion believe it will get them to heaven; some even believe their religion is the only way they can get there.

What is religion? It is an organized system of beliefs, rites and celebrations centered on a supernatural being; being pursued with devotion. Does any human being have the right to judge another person's beliefs and religion, or is God the only one who has this right? Does one church have the right to judge all other churches? Is it the church that saves a person's soul or is it his personal relationship with his Creator? Does the name on any church save a person's soul?

Have Americans become so educated that they know more than God the Creator? A few days back I talked to a preacher and he wanted to know what tribe I was from. I said Cherokee and he said that he had Cherokee blood. I told him I would be going to a Sun Dance in the Black Hills of South Dakota and that it was a very spiritual gathering. His remark was, "I don't believe in that." I said no more. How can you believe or not believe in something you know nothing about?

Maybe he had read or heard that they pierce the skin in this ritual and that it would be a sin to harm your body. Is it not a sin to pierce your ears for earrings that most women wear along with some of the men? Is it not a sin to harm your body by tattooing it all over? Is it not a sin to eat too much and become a glutton? Is it not a sin to smoke cigarettes that harm your body? Is it not a sin to run to the doctor to get medicine that will harm your body? Is it not a sin to buy meats from the grocery store that have been pumped full of chemicals that will do much more harm to your body? It looks to me like that it is only a sin if you are a Native American Indian.

The way I see things is that white people go to church three times a week for an hour or two. If the preacher's sermon goes over thirty to forty minutes the people get restless and begin to squirm in their seats. They are tired and thinking about that big plate of food at the restaurant and for this they have served the Lord well.

The first thing Indians do to worship the Creator at the Sun Dance is to go get a cottonwood tree selected by the elders. The tree is put in the middle of the dance circle. When cut, this tree cannot touch the ground. It is hauled back to the circle where it is decorated with ribbons and other things. Ropes are tied high upon the tree for the sun dancers who will be pierced, and then it is lifted up and placed into a previously dug hole in the middle of the circle. This tree acts as the altar where they do some of their praying.

The second day dancing begins. The dancers cannot eat or drink anything for the next four days that they dance. They dance into the circle for an hour or longer without stopping, then they take a break by going into the teepee to rest. There is a huge teepee for the women and one for the men. This is also where they sleep.

Break is over when the chief calls them back into the circle to dance again. Some of the men volunteer to be pierced while the other men and women keep dancing. To pierce this person or persons, they bring in a buffalo rug for the person to lie down on. Two slits are cut into each side of his chest, then a bone is run through the slits on each side of his chest with the ends sticking out far enough for the rope to cover each side. He then backs up until the rope is tight and pulls at his chest. He then begins to dance. He goes to the tree, places his hands on it and prays to his Creator. He makes a trip to the tree four times to pray. On the fourth time after praying he runs backwards as fast as he can so the bone will break through the flesh. If it doesn't break through he goes back to the tree and prays again. This is repeated until the flesh is broken, and as blood runs down his body he continues to dance until it ends.

114

Sometimes, up to four do this at the same time. They also have a buffalo skull pull which takes place by piercing the back shoulders the same way as they did the chest. Those who do this pull from four to ten buffalo skulls at a time, a very hard and demanding thing to do.

The last dance on Friday lasted a very long time. Some were pierced for the dance inside the circle and some were pierced for the buffalo skull pull outside the circle. After that a marriage ceremony took place in the circle and all this time the dancers had to keep dancing. It must have been a great relief for them when it ended.

This is all done to honor, praise and thank the Lord for giving them a life. The dancers do not look for any glory. It is a very spiritual thing. All the glory goes to God the Creator. They come close to feeling the pain and suffering that Christ went through; more so than anyone else in this country.

When white people do things that harm their body, they do it for pleasure. When the Indian does things that cause harm and pain to their bodies, they do it for the love of the Creator.

When meeting Chief American Horse, he asked if I was going to do a flesh offering. I told him I was thinking about it. He let me know when it was time, so I did it and am glad to know that some of my flesh was left at the base of the tree in the middle of the circle because it's done for the love and honor of the Creator.

At one time they invited anyone who wanted to come to the tree and pray as they were welcome. I sure wanted to be one of the many that walked into the circle and laid hands on the tree. My leg had been burning and hurting pretty bad but as I lay my hands on the tree and began to pray for others, the pain in my leg went away. Walking out of the circle I felt better than I had in years, so don't tell me that God was not there.

The people at the Sun Dance were some of the friendliest I have ever been around. Thanks to Sean and Yvette Collins for inviting me. I will be eternally grateful to them and can honestly say this was one of the best weeks I have had in a long time. All I can say is, "Thank You, Lord."

We Need to Band Together

All Indian tribes need to band together to make one strong nation. This includes federal, state, non-recognized tribes and everyone who believes they have a drop of Indian blood in their veins. Indian people can see that this country is not headed in the right direction and there are many people looking for a better way of living.

There are many here that are sick and tired of what's happening in our country; sick of filthy television shows and cussing, raw sex, brutal killings and murders on television and in the movies. They are looking for a better way to live.

Indian people did the things that were right and pleasing to the Creator when they occupied this country and the Europeans came here doing all the things that were wrong. Their hearts were filled with greed for money and power and they've just about destroyed a once clean and beautiful land that will soon be unable to sustain life as we know it.

Federal and state recognized tribes cannot do this alone. It will take all the tribes working together, even the wannabe Indians. We could be a power strong enough that the federal government would have to listen to our demands but if the Indians don't do it, this country is headed for total destruction.

Greed, brought here by Europeans, is the most destructive disease ever to hit this country. People think cancer and heart troubles are the biggest killers, but if people don't learn to control the greed in their hearts it will surpass all other diseases as the largest killer of mankind.

People living here today, if you care anything about your children, grandchildren and great grandchildren yet to be born, you had better wake up and take a look at where our country is headed because if you don't, your children's children will probably hate you because you left them with nothing.

In the near future I predict big changes coming and hope and pray that it is the Indian people becoming more in control. To me, they are the only race that can make things right according to God's will.

In my heart, God has been waiting for the Europeans to make amends with the Indians and He has sent many warnings for them, but

He sees no changes. To me, He is about ready to pick His Indian people up and put them back in charge of His creation.

No matter what happens here in this country, people must realize that changes need to take place before it gets to the point of no return. I see an angry God that is fed up with the way people do and act in this country.

If it's left up to the Europeans, this country won't get any better because they are the ones who got us into this mess. It makes little difference what the American people think, Indians, a race that has always looked to the Creator for guidance, are our only hope.

The Red Road

When most people hear the Indian phrase, "I'm walking the Red Road," they think they have some kind of cult going on. Many think Indians are a backward and ungodly bunch but let me tell you what *Walking the Red Road* means and then compare it to your religion. Then if you must judge us, judge us for what we truly are.

The Red Road is a term used frequently which means to live a traditional lifestyle: drug and alcohol free, respect for others, respect for yourself, respect for all living things, respect for creation and to worship the Creator, Great Spirit, Great Mystery—It means to walk among mainstream America alert and aware of the fact that you are very different than they are—and that is okay.

It means they will always try to make you the same as them because they are uncomfortable with your existence as an American Indian.

Always walk in a good way. Let them be reminded of lies told, treaties broken and promises made but do all you can to heal yourself and others. Keep your mind free and alert. Stay away from drugs and alcohol. Seek wisdom.

Attain peace in your heart and gift it to others in turmoil. We have never been and cannot be what they are—it's not in our blood. Stay strong, stay alive and give our children a future of confidence and pride.

We find no answers in material possessions—seek spiritual growth—find contentment and walk in the Creator's Light.

If you are not living up to the standards of the Red Road, why ask us to join your religion? Many think their religion is the only way to get to heaven. How you can feel this way? There are good people in all churches and God loves them. Many people don't respect God's creation because if they did, we would not see our rivers, streams and highways full of all kinds of garbage.

The largest race of people in America today is very critical of all other races, including many members of all churches. The Bible tells us to love everyone and just think how much better things would be if we could do that.

There were probably over five hundred nations of Indians living here before the Europeans came. They all spoke different languages and had different names for the Creator but they all had the same spiritual beliefs. This tells me that God the Creator had been in touch with these people long before another race came here.

The Great Spirit is where they received their guidance to live a life pleasing to the Creator. They were the only people who lived in harmony with all things on this earth.

Just a thought—"We have become a country that can find fault in everyone but ourselves."

The Time Has Come

The great state of Tennessee has come forward and done something that should have been done many years ago. Tennessee has apologized to the Cherokee and all other tribes in the Southeast for their part in the removal of Indians from this part of the country.

Tennessee was the first state that needed to apologize because the instigator of the tragedy was Andrew Jackson, a native of Tennessee and President of the United States, well known for killing Indians, along with several other presidents.

Since Tennessee finally decided to do the right thing it is now time for other states in the Southeast to do likewise. Some may think they don't need to apologize but they do. I would hate to be a political leader, state or federal, going to meet the Creator without making amends with Native Americans.

Our ancestors did the Indian people a great wrong and injustice and so far most people who now claim this land have never tried to correct those mistakes. Instead, they have sat back and watched the government still treat the first natives as if they are nothing. Most don't even realize that these are God's people and our brothers and sisters.

The State of Tennessee and leaders at the state capital in Nashville have my thanks for having enough goodness in their hearts to do the right thing. It is my prayer that other states will come forward and do the same; something they should have done years ago.

Every state in this nation has an obligation to Indian people and until that debt is repaid, I would not call this a Christian nation because I don't believe God sees it that way. God loves all people no matter what their color.

Racism, hatred and greed are three things that God cannot tolerate, so if we live with any of these three things in our hearts, then we are no better than the first Europeans that came here. These three things have caused all the problems we now have in this country.

It will not only be the first intruders who came here and killed Indians and stole their lands that will have to answer to God. Many people will have to answer to God for the way Indians have to live on reservations. God never intended for his little children to go to bed hungry and cold during the winter months on reservations—but they do.

Every day I thank God for letting me see the light years ago as to what I needed to do for the Indians. God's presence is felt any time I visit the Pine Ridge Reservation. I thank Him for being at the Sun Dance this year in South Dakota. When God looks into the faces of the dancers with their arms raised and looking straight at Him, I am sure He sees the love in their hearts for Him. He bled on the cross for them and they love Him enough to bleed for Him. No greater love can a person have. If everyone loved God as much as He loves us, there would be no problems.

The Pow Wow

The Pow Wow is a gathering of Indian people to dance, drum and sing praises to the Creator. If any have Indian blood in their veins and have never been to one and heard the beating of the drums, then they don't know how it feels to be Indian. For a long time I've known of my Indian blood, but didn't know how an Indian is supposed to feel until attending my first pow wow. An unbelievable feeling came over me; like having all my Indian ancestors there to greet me.

The drum beat is the heart beat of the Indian nation and the flute music gives one a feeling of peace and tranquility. Seeing all the dancers dressed in their colorful regalia dancing around the circle to the beat of the drums helps us feel that they are receiving a blessing from the Creator.

The dance circle is smudged with white sage, sweet grass, cedar or tobacco but mostly white sage. This is to cleanse and purify it; to make it ready for the dancers. In turn each dancer is smudged before entering the circle to get rid of any bad thoughts or feelings so they can enter with a pure heart. Then they can dance in the sacred circle with a clean heart and open mind to receive God's blessings.

When the dancing begins, the first to enter the circle are special people bearing the eagle's staff, the American flag, and the P.O.W. (Prisoner of War) flag along with other flags. After making a circle around the ring, they post the colors. Next they ask all soldiers and veterans present, along with policemen and medical professionals to come into the circle. After that the drum team plays a veteran's song.

When the first dance is completed, the dancers line up on both sides of the entrance to the circle which is always on the east. They hug and thank each soldier, veteran, policeman and medical people as they leave the circle in a very touching ceremony. The veterans feel that they have received more honors here at the pow wow than anywhere else.

The pow wow lasts all weekend and yes, we do have a church service on Sunday morning at most of them. It's not a hell fire and brimstone type sermon but someone tells what God has done for them in their life and there is a lot of talk about saving our Mother Earth. I feel the Lord's presence at a pow wow more so than anywhere else.

There are many vendors set up to sell their goods. Most of their items are handmade by the Indians and many hours are required to make many of them.

We are just one big family coming together to celebrate and thank the Creator for all the goodness He has bestowed upon us.

There are people who drive by during a pow wow and make unkind comments like: "Look at those crazy Indians out there dancing and carrying on! They must be drinking fire water!"

If you don't know what we are doing and don't want to stop and find out, then be very careful of whom you judge. They just might be some of God's chosen few and besides we don't make comments about your religion.

These are just my comments and others have their own opinions and that is good but I can tell you this, every time I go to a pow wow no matter where it takes place, it feels as though I have come home to meet some of my ancestors. Maybe that's the way an old Indian is supposed to feel.

Christmas on the Reservations

On the reservations out West, winters are especially harsh and brutal. The winds blow most of the winter with average temperatures hovering in the single digits and many times below zero. If you have ever been on a reservation, you can see that wood is very scarce. This is what many try to heat their homes with, along with heating oil which is very expensive. Their homes are very dilapidated and run down and very hard to heat; many without electricity or running water.

Indian people live very coldly in the winter months. Many children sleep on a mattress on the floor in drafty rooms, without enough blankets to keep them warm. Sometimes when it is extremely cold, some actually burn their furniture to keep themselves from freezing. There is always the danger of catching a cold or even pneumonia; the risk is especially dangerous without enough food in their stomachs.

It is a tragedy for these young children, as well as their grandmas and grandpas, to have to live in these conditions and suffer so much. Most of the American people don't realize that there are more Indians per capita that fight in the wars that keep America free; more than any other race. The Navajo Code Talkers are one of the main reasons we defeated the Japanese and before that the American military used the Choctaw Indian Code Talkers in the war against Germany. The Indians have been a great assistance in all the wars Americans have fought in. They just never seem to the get the credit and glory they deserve except with their own people. There they are treated for what they are on the reservations—heroes.

Indian children on the reservations are just like children everywhere. They get excited around Christmas time, even though many never get anything, but that's a way of life for them. They go to bed on Christmas Eve hoping there will be something for them on Christmas morning but most of the time they get nothing. Picture a little boy or girl Christmas morning, sitting at the table with tears in their eyes. They not only didn't get anything for Christmas, there is no food on the table to eat. When they are in school they get a good breakfast in the morning and a good lunch and for many the next meal they get is breakfast at school the next day. At home on weekends and holidays food is not always available. There are many children that don't get to go to school.

If the American people today would just think about what the Native people have been through and realize that they lost everything because of the Europeans and U. S. Government. Do you not think that it is about payback time? Just look at your families. Would you like for them to be living like the people on the Pine Ridge Reservation? I don't think so.

I am sure the Indian people would like to buy each other gifts and get things for their children at Christmas, but with unemployment running eighty to ninety percent, they people cannot do the things they would like to do. If not for a few caring people buying food and clothing and a few gifts for the children, it would be hard for them to survive in our world of today. If this is a Christian country, how can a tragedy like this happen?

Yes, Christmas on the reservation is a very sad time for most children, but there are happy times. It is sad for the children that don't get anything, and for the family's that don't have enough food, clothing or blankets. Even though they are the poorest people in the United States, they give thanks to the Creator every day for what He has blessed them with. Yes, you can be happy and still be poor.

The things that make me happy on Christmas morning are to know that I have supplied food for an entire family on the Navajo Reservation on Christmas Day. This includes a twenty pound turkey along with all the trimmings for a complete meal and maybe a toy for the children. Along with helping other organizations that help feed the poor on the reservations, to me this is what Christmas is all about. I would be afraid to face my God if I had not tried to help feed the poorest people in this country.

Merry Christmas to all, and may your teepee's be warm.

A Simple Solution to a Big Problem

The Poarch Band of Creek Indians has offered to solve the State of Alabama's deficit crisis with a two hundred and fifty million dollar advance. If our state government doesn't accept this offer, you can bet there will be many cuts in the health care and other programs. On top that that, there will be a tax increase.

Maybe our governor and other elected officials don't want to take money from what they consider a lower class of people. Just remember the Poarch Band of Creek Indians know how to operate a business and turn a profit. Our state government can't even keep their heads above water with all the money they receive from tax payers. Maybe the people of Alabama need to elect the Poarch Creek Indians to run our government and send the state politicians to the casinos and see how long it will take them to go broke.

The Poarch Creek Indians have been helping the State of Alabama for many years. They are a people that love this state and country; along with all the state recognized tribes in Alabama. They want to do what's best for our Mother Earth.

The two hundred and fifty million in advance is just the beginning. They are prepared to share a portion of their business revenue with the state—funds that will ensure Alabama's long term financial security.

To me, this sounds like the right thing to do. I have always thought it would take Indian people to get this country back on the right track and in the future, I see a Native American Indian as President of the United States of America.

Now if our elected officials in Montgomery would get off their high horses and stop thinking they are God's superior race and take some advice and the money from the only true Americans, things might just get better.

Spiritual Ways of Native Americans

Since I have been learning and following the spiritual ways of the Native American Indians, I now see why God loves them so much. Indian people don't wait until Sunday, Sunday night and Wednesday night to worship the Creator. For them it is a daily process; they pray and give thanks whenever they want to and the need arises.

Native people knew there was a higher power long before Europeans landed on the shores of this country. They referred to Him as the Great Spirit or Creator. Everything they did began with a prayer. Animals they killed for food, shelter and clothing were prayed over after the kill and thanks were given to the Creator.

They were people that never knew about money. There was never a need for it. For food they grew vegetables, killed animals for meat and traded for everything else they might need. They were very happy people with loving families and a way of life that had endured for thousands of years without much change in their lifestyle. Why would you want to change a good thing?

No one really knows how the Indians came to be in this country. There has been much speculation about their existence. My belief is that the Creator put them here in this country as caretakers of this land and that He gave them instructions on how to treat and take care of it and they did this for thousands of years.

Native Indians have some different views about how to serve and worship the Creator. Some other races look down on some of the things they do, especially the whites. I would be very careful about judging other people. I had a preacher tell me one day that he did not believe in that mess they do at the Sundance. After that his church was torn up by a tornado.

You go into your church to worship your god and that is good. Indians go into the sweat lodge to pray to the Creator and sweat poisons out of their body, yet you see us as doing wrong. Indian people don't waste time talking about other religions but you can bet that most all churches in this country talk about every other denomination and every other kind of religion.

You have different preachers come to your church to hold (the big meeting) and that is good to get other's views. Indian's come together to have the Sundance which is a very spiritual event. They fast for four days while dancing four times a day. Each dance lasts an hour and a half. During this time they pray to the Creator. Some men get pierced on each side of the chest, and then a bone is put through one slit and out the other slit. Next a rope is placed over each end of the bones on each side of the chest. They back up and bleed and suffer the pain. They do this because the Savior bled for them.

What really amazes me is the fact that this country was just as clean and unspoiled the day the Europeans showed up as it was the day of Indian's existence. They had no diseases until the white man showed up. Now we wonder why we have so many diseases, why the weather is so bad, why there are so many killings. There is one answer to all of our problems but it is so simple; people have become so highly educated they overlook it. You sure won't find it on those filthy television shows or dirty movies. You have to bow your head or look up toward the heavens to find the answer.

I Wanna Come Home

Have you ever wondered or even care about what a soldier's last words might be when on the front lines fighting the enemy? No, it was not all the cursing and bad language that the movies or television portrays. It is kind of funny how much the movie makers think they know about wars. They nor the actors who portray soldiers have probably never experienced it. He will first make peace with his God. Then his words will be, "I wanna go home and see my family and friends one more time."

There have been many soldiers saying 'I wanna go home" right before they get killed. Home and family are the most important things and what's on their minds right before they die. Many of the soldier's last words are "Momma, I wanna come home."

Being a soldier on the frontline is a very lonely place. Even though you have some of your buddies and friends around you, they can't take the place of your loved ones and home. Home is what's on every soldier's mind when he thinks he might get killed.

Many people at home don't ever think about a situation like this, because they have never been in service and never had any of their immediate family in the military. To them, military service is for other people. They reap all of the rewards that come from freedom that others fight and die for. They are probably the ones that never say 'thank you' to a soldier or veteran.

Many in this country take freedom for granted. They think freedom is a privilege that comes to people living here, so they will never volunteer to go to another country to fight so we in America can stay free. Many would not even fight if war broke out in our own country.

The only reason we now enjoy freedom in this country is because many soldiers died on the battlefields in other countries to give us this freedom and many of their last words were, "Momma, I wanna come home." My thinking is that God carried them to their eternal home where they will suffer no more and wait for Momma and loved ones to come to their final home.

What I see in the near future is that wars will be fought by hackers on the internet. I wonder how people will feel when they shut our country down. We will probably be the first it will happen to because most other countries hate us. How will we feel about all of this high technology when we can't buy groceries, gasoline or anything else? Will it be worth it then or will we think back to the good old days when God was still in control? We won't be saying, "Momma, I want to come home." We will be asking God to come back and save our country.

The Creator has given us so many opportunities to begin doing what is right. There will come a day when we will ask for His help. He might tell us it's too late.

Our Mother Earth

When I was a very young boy living in the community where I grew up, I could see all the beauty that God had created. It was amazing to walk out in the woods or down on the creek and river banks and see the wild animals, birds and clean waters. It was a pure pleasure just to look at beautiful trees, smell wildflowers and the freshness of the air. It was a paradise for sure.

When I was young, I learned that I had Indian blood in my veins and as I grew older, I began to learn the truths about the Indian people. It was sure not what our history books had taught us. The older I became, the more I learned making my Indian blood run hot in my body. It was a big cover up the Europeans tried to pull off and it worked for many years, but not anymore.

Native American Indians and Europeans are very different in their beliefs and religion. The Indian can look out across this land and see something very different than the European does. The first thing the Indian sees is our Mother Earth, something the Creator created and for that reason it is considered sacred ground to them. They believe that everything that was created is to be respected and they are connected to all of His creation. Not only humans have spirits but all living things do.

They worshipped the Creator long before any other race came here with their Bibles. It makes one wonder if they knew something already that the whites had to have a Bible to learn. You can be assured that Indians knew how to take care of the Creator's creation. They did what the Creator expected all people to do, yet the majority of American's still looks down on them and believes they should stay consigned to the reservations.

What does the white man see when he looks out across this land? He sure doesn't see this earth as His mother. He sees a land full of raw materials that can make him plenty of money. The trees are beautiful but we need to cut them for lumber. All the land he sees, he wants to purchase and get a title to it. His dream is about all the money he can make. He does not think about the future generations and what he will leave them. His thoughts are, I got to get while the getting is good.

Indian people use the Creator's creation for his church. They pray about everything they plan to do. They pray over each animal they kill for food and thank the Creator for providing it. An old Indian saying is, "The white man goes in his church and prays to His God; the Indian goes into his teepee and talks to the Creator.

No matter who you are, or how you feel about our Mother Earth, we all need to take care of it so future generations won't have to try to live on a dead planet.

Joey and Rory

Ever since I first saw Joey and Rory on the RFD network about two years ago, I saw something different about this couple. You can just see the love they have for each other, the love they have for this country and their fellowman, and you can see and hear the loyalty to God and this country in the music they sang.

Many country singers today are in the business just to make money. They all sound about alike and their music sounds about the same. Most of them are not in it because they love it.

Joey and Rory are naturals; plain and simple in their approach to entertaining people. Believe me; this country needs more of their kind of entertainment and you will never hear them sing anything that is not good for children to hear.

Although I have never met them, they are at the top of the list of my favorites. This country needs a lot more entertainers with the same values these two have.

A lot of music nowadays has kind of followed television and gone to the dogs. This is why Joey and Rory and their music is so important in today's world. I believe they will always keep their standards high and for that God will bless them greatly.

My Indian friend in Florence, Alabama, Yvette Collin was with child the same time Joey was carrying her baby. Yvette's baby was born in a teepee there on their farm delivered by a midwife. I know Joey used a midwife from The Farm near Summertown, Tennessee.

Yvette and Joey remind me a lot of each other. Joey is into her music and Yvette is into teaching other women the spiritual ways of Native Americans. They even remind me in their similar looks. To me Joey looks to have Indian blood. Maybe someday they will even get to meet each other.

Joey and Rory, I don't believe you need to change a thing about your music. I think the American people are looking for exactly what you have. This country needs to get back to loving what God created for His people, and looking to Him for all of our answers.

Rory, I am not forgetting your daughter, Heidi, also one of my favorites. I have stopped by Marcy Jo's for breakfast a few times but have never been able to meet any of you, and that's okay. I don't have to meet you to enjoy your music and I would say just keep your music honest and down to earth simple.

A Godfather

Thinking about a godfather figure never crossed my mind much but I thought you had to be someone very special to be asked to become one. Gangster movies were made about godfathers, but they were godfathers of mobsters, racketeers, and thieves, and should have been named "devil fathers" because there was nothing right about gangsters.

The first Sundance I ever attended was because Sean and Yvette Collin invited me to go. Yvette was with child, but she danced every dance, an unbelievable task for a pregnant woman.

About three months later, she gave birth to a beautiful baby boy in a teepee there on their farm. A little later they called me saying they wanted to talk to me, so I met them at Big Spring Park in Tuscumbia during the return to the Coldwater Indian Festival.

They asked me if I would be the godfather of their little boy, Nakota Braveheart Collin. Speechless for a few seconds I then said, "Yes. It would be a great honor." Then she laid Nakota in my arms and said you are the first to hold him outside the family.

No one could ever know the feeling in my heart at that moment. It was a huge surprise and one of the biggest thrills of my life. My thoughts at that moment were how much God has blessed me during my lifetime. The Collin family has been very special to me ever since our first meeting. I love them like my own family and believe they feel the same about me because they asked me to be a grandpa to their other children, Huyanha and Cruz.

My pledge to Sean and Yvette is that I will be the best godfather and grandpa to their children I can possibly be. I will love them as my own and try my very best to be a good role model for them to look up to, with the hope that they will remember me in a good way after I leave this earth.

The Collin family is the most spiritual people (this includes Yvette's brother Mark) that I have ever been associated with. Yes, they dance in the Sundance because our Savior bled for us on the cross; in return they bleed for Him. Yes, they do the sweat lodge because it's like a church where they pray and sweat to cleanse their body and yes, they put the Creator first in their lives. The Creator puts a few special people on this earth to help show other people the right path to follow and for me this family is at the top of that list.

You would really have to know them before you could understand why I speak so highly of them. One thing that really amazes me is that anytime I am around them, I feel the presence of our Lord. That is a great feeling.

Our Government

When a veteran, along with other concerned citizens, has to beg for money to help other veterans who are disabled, many living on the streets begging for something to eat, then something is very wrong with the government we have today.

You politicians in Washington find it very easy to send our troops to foreign countries all over the world to fight other people's wars but let them get their legs, arms or something else blown off; then wants to ignore and forget about them.

If you were a government for the people you would take care of these soldiers for the rest of their lives. If you can't afford to do that, quit sending them to fight other people's wars! You might also stop sending those foreign countries billions of dollars of taxpayers' money every year, and then you would have money to take care of our veterans.

A government that will not take responsibility for the young men and women it sends to other countries wars over and over again until their lives are destroyed is not a government that neither works for nor cares about its people.

The politicians in Washington think it is right to keep sending the same ones multiple times to a war zone but I bet if you had to lead them into these battles you would not be so eager to go. A soldier should only have to go to a war zone one time. If it was your son or daughter, you would find a way not to send them at all.

What you pay the soldiers who fight and die for this country is at the bottom of the pay scale, but they only fight and die for your freedom here in America. Pro ball players and movie stars make millions of dollars every year, but they supply you with entertainment and that's what you enjoy. They are heroes to your kids but never do anything for the freedom of our country.

I am not against anyone making big money, but I am against a government that won't take care of the ones who fight and die to keep our freedom.

Why don't you have some of these soldiers without arms or legs come to the White House and tell their story instead of hiring some high priced entertainer to come and sing to you? I'm sure the soldier's story would be worth more than a song or two. You might help someone who needs the money.

Daniel Webster said, ". . . I am committed against everything which, in my judgment may weaken, endanger, or destroy the Constitution and especially against all extension of executive power, and I am committed against any attempt to rule the free people of this country by the power and the patronage of the government itself."

Thomas Jefferson said, "I, however, place economy among the first and most important republican virtues, and public debt as the greatest of dangers to be feared to preserve our independence, we must not let our rulers load us with perpetual debt . . . I am for a government rigorously frugal and simple."

John Adams said, "Our Constitution was made only for a moral and religious people. It is wholly inadequate to the government of any other."

Benjamin Franklin said, "Only a virtuous people are capable of freedom. As nations become corrupt and vicious, they have more need of masters."

Now I ask you, what kind of government do we have today?

Prejudice

Prejudice is a disease imbedded in most everyone's heart here in America. It does not matter if you are white, black, red or yellow; you still have it. It first came to this country when the first shipload of foreigners landed on the shores, along with every other kind of disease. It is the one thing that has caused many of our problems here.

All men are created equal. This does not mean that all will be white and look alike. When God said all are created equal, He was talking about when you are born. All newborn babies, male and female are without sin, hatred, greed or any other animosity. I believe somewhere in the Bible He says all people should be your brothers and sisters. Now I ask you, can you look at another colored person and see them as your brother or sister?

It is beyond my imagination why the white race thinks they are superior. Is it because Hitler tried to build a superior race in Germany? Is it because foreigners came into this country and killed most of the Native Indians and stole their land? In God's eyes, you are superior over nothing and if you can't look at other races and see them as brothers and sisters, then you are probably in big trouble.

Many preachers, along with their congregations, want a few of the different colored people in their church—but not too many; just enough for them to say they are not prejudiced. A church that will not let a person come into their place of worship because they think he is a sinner, is not dressed properly, or is the wrong color are in danger of losing their own souls. A person who tells another person they are going to hell is likewise in danger.

Even our government is very prejudiced but that is nothing new. They now work on ways to get rid of the Mexicans here. Many whites want them gone also. It is just too bad that the Indian people were not prejudiced when the Europeans first arrived here. If they had been, there might still have been only Indians living here.

If people could just have a change of heart and get rid of racial hatred, greed, prejudice and the love of money, I believe our God would work all kinds of miracles for us, but instead of this happening we seem to be headed in the other direction.

If you are someone that is in church every time the doors are open, but you are still prejudiced, think back to the time when your ancestors came here killing Indians and stealing their land. And you still look down on the red people because you have never done anything to correct your ancestor's mistakes. Don't you ever wonder how God feels about this?

They Will Suffer No More One Day

Last night was very cold with temperatures in the single digits. As I lay sleeping in the warmth of my bed, I suddenly awoke with something on my mind. I thought about the Indian people who were on that forced march known as The Trail of Tears. As I lay there trying to imagine how much they had to suffer it was a frightening experience.

If you think you realize just how much they had to suffer, then take one blanket with no shoes on, go outside and lie on the ground with the temperature below twenty degrees and see how long you can take it. Just maybe you might understand what they had to go through all winter long.

There is no way modern man could have survived the anguish and torture those Native Americans endured, never having enough clothes or blankets to keep themselves warm; some without shoes and never enough food to fill their stomachs. When the government began rounding them up, the weather was still warm and they had to leave with just the clothing they had on.

How could any human being let something like this happen to another human being? The problem was that white Europeans didn't consider them as being human. They even had the gall to proclaim that God told them to do this. Apparently God gave them the opportunity to be any kind of idiot they wanted to be.

Native American Indians were God's people. He gave them this land but the Europeans had a lust to kill and steal. They were very good at it. Many will have to answer to God for their wrongs.

Many who live today will have to answer to God for the way Indian people are still treated. The U. S. Government's reservations they forced them to live on still run rampant with white man's diseases, hunger and bitter cold winter, and I have not seen many people who really care.

One would think after all the years since the Indian wars that things might get better for those on the reservations but it's hard for a conquered people to rebound without the means and no help. But that's the way the government and European people keep them under control.

There will come a day of reckoning and God help those who have fallen short on their responsibilities. When God asks, "Why did you not help my first people? They have cried ever since they were put on those horrible reservations and you never offered to help, so don't tell me that you're in your church every time the doors are open and that you are praying for your soul every day. I expect a lot more out of my people and if Indian people cry from hunger, you are not doing what you are supposed to be doing.

"Your ancestor's were wrong when they came here killing my beloved people and stealing their land. And so far you have done nothing to correct their mistakes yet you want me to bless you.

"Indian people were and still are the greatest race to have lived on my creation. They did things right and pleasing to me. No European white person can ever come close to being what Indian people are to me because your hearts have drifted away from me and this earth. If you can't feel the heartbeat of our Mother Earth, then I might not even know you."

We Americans

We Americans need to realize where this country is headed and begin to stand up for what is right. We now let the politicians in our government, along with many other organizations, try very hard to lead us down the wrong path. This is a great country to live in and when our government was formed, it was the best in the world. For God's sake, don't judge our government by the politicians we have in office today.

The leaders of our country have drifted so far away from our constitutional rights that it makes one wonder if they are true believers in what is right. This country was founded on "in God We Trust". I sometimes wonder what happed to that belief. Have greed, hate, racism and love of money replaced what our country was founded on? When God the Creator has stated that it is wrong, then that's it. His word is the law. It does not matter how many new laws the government passes or how many churches change their rules to fit society. None of this will make it right. God stays the same. His rules stay the same; only the people change.

Even though this land was stolen from people that loved the Creator and love what He had created for them to live upon, they treated the land with the greatest respect. The newcomers didn't learn a thing about how to take care of this earth. I would think by now you could see where our country is headed.

There are many people and many organizations that are working very hard to turn us against God, the Creator. Some are the politicians in Washington. Television is probably the most influential of all with so few decent shows on anymore. If it was not for RFD network, I would not have television. I would love to see America get back to the way it was years ago. When politicians could be trusted and worked for the people who pay their salaries. When our flag was respected, stood for our freedom and was a symbol of devotion to our great country: when our God was in our schools, homes and all other public places; when prayer was allowed anywhere at any time, with no objection; when neighbors were your friends, not your enemies and when you could leave home without worries of getting back because of crime, murders or bad weather.

Progress is great and the way it should be with all the inventions that have made life so much easier, but for God's sake, don't forget who is in charge of the whole world. Never forget all the soldiers who fought and the many that died fighting for freedom in this country. What would you give or do to save our country?

Many people think that the reservations are the place for the Indian people. Have you ever thought about all the Indians that enlisted in our military to fight for this country? If it had not been for the Indian Code Talkers in World Wars I and II, those wars could have been lost. Just think. The Indian Code Talkers might have saved the world! Now think about the first Indian schools where children were forced to attend, not allowed to speak their own language yet their language may have saved the world. Our government has always made mistakes. They are even better at it today.

One Day I Woke Up

One day I woke up and the world seemed to have passed me by. It was as if I was in another world, nothing at all like the place I grew up in. How could things have changed so much in my lifetime? Sometimes the progress that has taken place is overwhelming. But like most other older people, I long for the good old days. It is a very lonely feeling knowing it will never be like that ever again.

As I grew up, neighbors were friends and sometimes kinfolk, but now days they are just strangers. What a joy it was to go visit our kinfolk; people we loved and wanted to be around. Now children don't even know who their kinfolk are. What a shame!

Kids were very happy back then. We had to work, but when we had time off we took advantage of it. God's creation was our playground. What a joy to be down on the river fishing or in the woods hunting. When time allowed, we were camped out on the creek or riverbanks and cooked our own food. Now days if kids are not on the computer playing games, they are bored and I bet that ninety percent of them don't even know what a tadpole is or a flying Jenny or a slingshot or a rabbit trap or a crawfish. Do you even know how to skin a cat?

What happened to the happy times we enjoyed growing up? Kids today will never learn the happiness we knew because of all the progress that has come about. You have cell phones today. We had two tin cans with a string coming from the middle of each can to talk through. You have HD (High Definition) television to watch; we had radios to listen to the Grand Ole Opry on Saturday night. You go to the movies; we went possum hunting. You pick up your date in a car; we walked to see our girlfriends. You listen to rap music; we listened to the owls, whippoorwills and bullfrogs. Do kids of today even know that there are stars up in the sky with all kinds of formations to pick out?

Do you think milk comes from the grocery store? We knew it came from a cow because we had to do the milking. You think you can't live without the computer and internet; we lived without electricity in our homes for a time. You get up at night and go to the bathroom; we got up and went to the outhouse about fifty yards away from the house. When you get out of school, you are on vacation; when we got out of school, we went to the fields to pick cotton, pull corn or bale hay.

Yes, things have changed. People now live the easy life and think it is the best way, but I have my doubts. As I think back to my school days, I can remember that there were only two overweight kids in the entire school. I believe it was because our work around home never ended. Another thing I remember is that we never seemed to go to a doctor. Any time we were a little sick, my mom always had a remedy that worked better than the medicine they have today. One of the things I see in today's world is that people are drifting away from our Creator and for that reason bad things now happen.

American Pride

American pride was at its strongest during World War I and World War II. The American people knew that the men and women fighting in foreign countries fought for our freedom here in the United States. People were proud to fly the American flag. In most schools, children placed their hand over their heart and recited the Pledge of Allegiance to the Flag, followed with a prayer each morning. Most families placed a star in the window for each family member that was in the military.

Upon returning home, each soldier was treated as what they truly were; heroes. The United States loved and respected all the soldiers returning home and many parades were held to honor them. People grieved for those that lost their lives so that we could live free here.

Great sacrifices were made by soldiers and also the people at home. Some things like sugar and gasoline were rationed but we were Americans and we could deal with the hardships that came during those wars. Things got better after World War II. More jobs opened up and some made more money though there were still many without work who struggled to get by.

The year was 1950 and the Conflict in Korea had begun. Communist North Korea invaded South Korea. America, along with its allies, stepped in to help South Korea. Many National Guard units were called into active duty service including the one that four of us boys in the same class in high school had joined. Although we knew we were going to miss our senior year, we knew it was our duty to go and help the South Koreans.

After 13 months in Korea, we were on our way home, feeling good about what we had accomplished. We were filled with American pride. When we arrived home, outside our families, there was no 'thank you,' no 'glad you're home,' no 'good to see you.' It was as if American pride died while we were gone.

It was worse for American soldiers who fought in Viet Nam. There was a lot of protesting during that war especially among college students. They had been in college just long enough to become idiots. Where would those students have been if not for the soldiers that had fought and died for their freedom?

Yes, it seems like the American spirit and pride has fallen by the wayside. Can we blame it on our government? They have let the American people down, but who votes these jerks into office? I think the American people just love liars.

People, we are headed in the wrong direction. We have almost let the government take God out of our lives. Now we let them make laws that go against what He teaches and we still wonder why there is so much destruction in our world. There is only one simple answer; God is angry at the people.

If we don't get God back in our daily lives and stand up for what is right, things will get worse. We need to get our enemy out of the White House. For God's sake, don't let the government tell you where and when you can pray. Prayer is about the only hope we have.

This was a good, decent place when God was allowed in our country. To me God's biggest enemies here are television, the internet and our government.

My Heart Bleeds

A few years ago, I had the opportunity to go out west and go through some of the Indian reservations. What I saw was a third world condition right here in the United States. I have been going back for the last few years traveling through the Pine Ridge Reservation and what I see makes my heart bleed.

People that once were the greatest race the Creator ever put in this country is what I see. God the Creator intended for them to be caretakers of this land. He gave them a pure, clean country without any form of diseases. They did not even have an immune system because there was no need.

For thousands of years they lived the good life, looking to the Creator for guidance daily. What the intruders did to them was nothing short of a holocaust or genocide. They had the gall to claim that God had told them this was the right thing to do, the most idiotic statement I ever heard.

The U. S. Government broke every treaty they made. They killed them, stole their land, beat them down, and penned them up like animals. They brought all kinds of diseases. It was their goal to get rid of them completely, a very strange way for a so-called Christian people to act. If there have ever been people in this country that has been true to what the Creator expects of His people, it is the Native American Indians.

I wouldn't want to be one of those Christians that go to church every time the doors are open, wear fine clothes, drive new cars, go out to eat, then go back to big fine homes while ignoring what the Bible says in Proverbs 21:13, "Whoever shuts his ears to the cry of the poor will also cry himself and not be heard."

There is no other race in this country that suffers more than Indians on the reservation. They sleep cold in the winter months, hot in the summer months; and go hungry most of the time. I could not sleep at night if I did not do what I can to help them.

I am proud of the Indian blood that runs through my body but sometimes ashamed of the other kind since I have been following the spiritual ways of native Indians and have grown much closer to my God the Creator. Now I look at other people as my brothers and sisters no matter the color of their skin.

Every year I purchase an entire meal for a family on the reservations including a 16-18 pound turkey with all the trimmings, canned vegetables and fruits to make pies, even coffee and fruit drinks; everything they need to make a complete meal plus a toy for the youngsters. The cost is only $58.60. This is one thing that makes me feel good.

Christmas for me is not about getting; it is about giving to people in need and there is no other race in need as much as Native Indians. I am for churches and the great works they do. More power to them, but I sometimes wonder what their most important goals are with the offerings taken. Does any of the money help feed the poor in this country or does it all go to pay for those fancy churches and the good salaries of the preacher or maybe foreign missions? I am not against any of this but just trying to let you know that there is a desperate need on these reservations.

Indian people walk to their sweat lodge, go in and sit on the ground. They sweat the poisons out of their body and talk to the Creator and thank Him for what He has blessed them with. The other race gets in his big fine car, goes to his big fine, air conditioned church, sits on padded seats and prays to God for something he wants or needs. It makes me wonder which meeting God attends.

Having no dislike for anyone, I love all people no matter what name is on the building where they worship. God doesn't look at the name of a building; He looks at what's in your heart.

My intent is not to offend anyone by my writings but my heart will bleed until the Native American Indians are treated for what they are; good God loving people that I am proud to call my brothers and sisters. Your white ancestor came here killing them and stealing their land. I wouldn't let too many more sunsets come and go before trying to make amends. Many will be held accountable for this catastrophe.

From Boys to Men

Along with three classmates at Clements High School in Limestone County, Alabama, I decided to join the local National Guard unit. It was the 1343rd Combat Engineers, Company B. We were sixteen years old. In the summer of 1949, we traveled to Fort Benning, Georgia for two weeks of training. The first morning in the mess hall for breakfast, it did not seem to matter that the cook frying our eggs also got sweat on them. We learned to eat whatever they dished out.

During the day, our training was in the swamps where the mosquitoes were as big as horse flies and the land was as springy as rubber. It was so hot you could see steam coming up out of the ground. We were country boys and had learned to work hard at a young age, so we tolerated the hot weather.

One night on a training mission, it was rainy and messy. It simulated real war. Guns fired and shells exploded, giving one an eerie feeling. The thing that concerned me most was being waist high water as I was sure it was full of snakes and alligators.

After returning home, we went back to our regular jobs, working in the fields. We entered the eleventh grade in 1949. Two of us played sports and were pretty good at it, having a great basketball season. In August of 1950, the four of us were about to begin our senior year but about two weeks before school began; we were notified to be at the National Guard Armory the next morning. The First Sergeant called the company to order. The company commander stood before us for a time and then said, "You are now active members of the United States military and your training will begin immediately.

We trained at the armory and the fairgrounds and after about two weeks, traveled to Fort Campbell, Kentucky for our basic training which was hard, fast and vigorous with long hours.

From there we loaded on a troop train and arrived in Seattle, Washington. A few days later we embarked on a ship, *The Mariene Phoenix*. Our first stop was Yokahama, Japan and then on to Pusan, Korea. After a few weeks, we boarded LSTs and headed up the coastline, landing at Inchon, a city that had been bombed to the ground. We traveled in trucks to Seoul- it had also been destroyed- and then headed north. It was not long until we heard the big guns firing and as we passed them, we knew exactly where we were going to be. We became men in a very short time.

We learned a lot about life while in Korea. Our families are the ones we missed most. We learned to love your country and the freedom we have. We also learned that freedom comes at a very high price. We boys were very proud of serving our country. We were in Korea for 13 months, most of it at the front lines.

All four of us made it through the war. I believe our Creator watched over us. We were in the Punch Bowl, where many men died, when we began rotation to go home. When we arrived home, besides our families, there were no 'thank yous', no 'glad you made it home', no nothing. It was as if we had never left home. We each knew what we had been through and what we had accomplished, so we walked tall and proud.

Clements High School finally decided to issue us our diplomas. We graduated with the class of 2015. You might say it took us 64 years to get through our senior year. The rest of our class finished in 1951. It was a great honor thanks to Jason Black and his wife Velvet; without them this never would have happened.

Why I Write Stories

Why do I write stories for the newspapers? It is because my God laid some things on my heart years ago. There is a race living in this country that has been wrongly treated ever since the first ship landed on our shores. What He laid on my heart was to help the Indian people in any way I could, and I will do that until the day I cross over.

The intruders treated the Indians like they were not even human beings stealing their lands and killing off most of them because they were a greedy, disrespectful kind of people who could only see a country filled with natural resources that could make them rich.

Killing Indians and stealing their land was natural for those who called themselves Christians. Those people had forgotten one thing: God gave them this land and they were among some of His most beloved people. They not only killed Indians and stole their land; many of them earned themselves a one way ticket to the other place.

Most people today don't think about Indian people living on reservations in horrible conditions. They just ignore them and don't want to hear about their situation. Most churches are too busy sending some of their congregation on foreign missions to think about the Indian people.

There are still many people living today that think like their ancestors did when they came here killing Indians. If you have this kind of feelings in your heart, I feel sorry for you. Just don't think that only white people go to heaven. If you can't learn to love and get along with all races, why do you even go to church? You are not learning God's word.

Attitudes today are one reason we are in such a terrible condition. They think only of themselves, their wants and desires. The reason I don't go to church regularly isn't because I don't like it. When one goes regularly, they expect you to pay tithes to that church and they make you feel obligated. I see a greater need in helping the hungry here in America, much more than sending some of their members on foreign missions. I feel the Indians on reservations face hunger problems more than anyone else. Now does that make you right and me wrong? I would not argue the point. I will just leave that up to my God.

I know a lot of people need to come down off their high horse and think about people in need. There are many folks that live high and mighty and don't have a clue to what life and hardships are all about. If you think that you are one of those righteous Christians who are in church every time the doors are open and think you can do no wrong but still look down at other races as unequal to you and don't want to have anything to do with them, you just might be serving the wrong God.

Many people in America do very well for themselves and their children get a good education. They have everything they need to have a good, comfortable life. Now think about the Indian people living on reservations. They have no hope for the future or that things will get better. Many go hungry and sleep cold in winter months. Unemployment runs about 90%. They live in rundown shacks for homes, many without water or electricity and not enough clothing nor blankets to keep them warm in the winter.

Now think about this. That big, fine home you live in and that property you have a deed for was stolen from the Native American Indians and you still call this a Christian nation.

My World

While I am not saying that the world I grew up in is better than the world we live in today, I am saying it was very different. Many will say that it is just the same. I will agree that it is the same place, but totally different in people's ways, views, beliefs and actions and also in the weather.

You might ask what is so different today. The first thing that comes to my mind is, we went from the horse and wagon days to the space age and all of the high tech gadgets that caused the destruction of a simple way of life.

In my world when we had health problems our parents used old timey ways and remedies to cure our ailments. Sickness in our family was very rare. People have become too smart to use the old remedies that worked so well for us. Now days they run to the doctor every time they sneeze. The doctor is more than happy to put them on some pills. When you go back for a recheck he will sell you more pills. Many older people today have to have a tote bag to carry all their pills and medicines in.

Growing up we never had store bought toys to play with. We made all the things we played with. We were outside kids, during both summer and winter. Why would we want to be inside? There was no computer, no television and not even radio for a short time. All the fun things to do were outside.

Some of the things we did know were where every good fishing hole on the river and creek was and every den tree where the squirrels lived and which fields the rabbits hid in. We also knew most of the names of trees and were very familiar with the trees and vines that supplied us with food. We never had to go hungry out in the woods and fields. There was always some kind of food around.

We knew and loved all our neighbors. What a joy it was to be around good people you enjoyed visiting with and sometimes sharing a meal. Most of my growing up years there was always kinfolk that lived close by. Back then everyone knew and loved all their kinfolk.

Christmas was a very special and joyous time for us, because we knew we our socks would be filled with oranges,, apples, nuts and hard candy. Kids today don't have to wait for Christmas. They get anything they want anytime they want. They don't know the joy of having to wait until Christmas to get simple things like oranges and apples.

Years ago people went to church to worship God and give praises to our Lord. Clothes were not a big issue. You wore what you had. Today many go to church to show off new clothes and new cars and to see what everyone else is wearing.

In my time, mothers cooked at home most every meal. For that reason, we ate healthy. Today they head to the restaurant to eat, not too healthy. Most mothers today don't even know how to cook.

Indian people watch as the majority of others destroy this earth, knowing that the Creator is not going to put up with this much longer. It's too bad that white America calls this a Christian nation and doesn't know the first thing about taking care of God's greatest gift—this earth. I loved the world I grew up in because we did not know about all the things that make young people happy today. I will continue to live my life as close to the world I grew up in because thoughts of that world still make me happy.

No matter what you think, do or talk about, there is only one answer to most of our problems and if you don't know the answer to that, problems are only going to get worse.

My Spiritual Ways

Years ago, I chose to follow the spiritual ways of Native American Indians. It is my opinion that their beliefs are far stronger than other religions today. My view of them is attending church every time the doors are open and paying tithes and for doing that you are a saved person. I believe my God, the Creator, expects much more of His people.

God's creation of this earth was one of His greatest gifts to human beings and it should be treated as sacred ground. The white man does not respect this earth. All he sees is a way to make money. Look at the roadsides, highways, rivers and many streams of water and see exactly how the majority feel about this earth.

146

Indian people believe that they are related to all living things. The white man believes that he is only related to his immediate family and sometimes don't even claim that. Because the Indians claim relation to all living things, they never kill anything except for food or clothing. Even when they kill an animal for food they pray over it and thank the Creator for supplying it. Did you ever see a white man praying over anything they killed? They do not kill for food; they kill for the trophies to hang on their walls.

The amazing thing about the American Indian is they never needed money until the white man showed up. There was no need for it and they were some of the happiest people that ever lived here.

It's hard to believe in a so-called Christian people that came into a new country trying to kill off the native people and steal their homelands, and then have the ignorance to claim that God told them to do this. The way I see that kind of people is as working for the devil killing Christians. Indians were the only ones doing what was right in God's eyes.

When I do go to a church I feel very uncomfortable with all those eyes looking at me. I guess they are sizing me up to see if I would fit in their congregation or checking to see what kind of clothes I have on.

Then again, when I go into a sweat lodge, I feel the presence of our Lord. We not only sweat the poisons out of our body, we talk to our God, mostly thanking Him for all the things He has blessed us with.

I have three of the most spiritual people I have ever know that I learned from Sean and Yvette Collin and her brother Mark. They are always upbeat; never down and out. They work for the Creator and He gives them the strength to do amazing things. They made me the godfather of their young son, Nakota and Grandpa to their other children Cruz and Huyanha. If you ever want to feel the presence of our Creator just be around this family for a short time. I consider them my family and I love them very much.

Another person that is very dear to my heart is Brother Tom Hendrix. He has accomplished more in his life time than anyone else except our Creator. The Rock Wall he built to honor his great great grandmother Te-Lah-Nay who walked the Trail of Tears to the Oklahoma Territory and then walked back to Alabama has drawn people from all over the world to see his wall.

One day, Tom told me about a church group that came to see the wall and while he explained how it came about, the preacher spoke up and said, "You know all the Indians that were here before the Bible came are gone to hell." Brother Tom said he stood there for a short time then told them they "were in the wrong place. You just need to leave." You just never know where an idiot will show up and wonder why a lot of people don't go to church.

Why would any church group want to judge another church? They know nothing about the feelings of the people in that other church. If you think God goes by the name on a church in being saved, then you might be the ones in trouble. It would be a sad situation if only one church group was in heaven.

Most churches judge each other; that's a problem. There is only one judge when it comes to getting to heaven. I am so proud that the Indian people don't judge other people. They just sit back and smile at this rat race in our country today. He sees the prominent race of people destroying this earth and themselves.

What If

Close your eyes and picture a people rounded up like animals and put in holding pens. They had to leave their homes with just the clothes they had on. Babies and women cried. Men were confused and did not know what was happening or why. When told they had to relocate out West, they did not understand. This had been their home and homeland for thousands of years.

Once most of them were rounded up, their homes and possessions burned, they began the long walk to their new homes out West, a land considered worthless and desolate but good enough for them. Much of the journey took place during the winter months.

These people were forced to leave everything behind and the land they had worked and loved would no longer be theirs. This was the worse treatment in this country any people have ever been subjected to.

There were a few wagons supplied by the government for some to ride in, but people were proud and refused. Not being able to bring extra clothing with them, this event turned into an unbearable situation as they endured a very harsh winter. They had walked so much their shoes had worn out; now their feet were freezing. Due to the lack of proper clothing their bodies stayed cold all the time. Trying to sleep on frozen ground without enough covers or blankets was a tragedy.

They walked every day without stopping to rest. This forced march took its toll on them. Many died every day. The food fed to them was nothing more than slop. I doubt if a hog would eat it. It made them sick. Many died from the bad food and many froze to death. Many more died from brutal beatings by the guards.

Many small babies died because mothers didn't get enough food to produce milk. Imagine a mother in tears watching her baby die as it starved to death. Old men fell by the wayside, unable to walk anymore. Some of the stronger men carried them on their backs until they died.

Many shallow gravesites were dug for the bodies of the many dying daily. The dead buried along the trail now numbered into the thousands.

Do you have a picture in your mind of just how bad these people were treated? Can you see the suffering they had to endure? What is so bad is that they still suffer on reservations.

Now think; what if this had been the white race? What if it was your people living on reservations out West today? Would you be willing to help them or would you treat them like you do the Indians?

Many people today have just lost caring for and about others. They only think of themselves. Most everyone in this country, whether they go to church or not, know what God expects of His people, but many will never heed before it's too late.

God wants everyone to treat each other as brothers and sisters. Can you do that? Can you treat Indians on the reservations as your brothers and sisters? When you cross over and God asks you, "Why did you not help my people on those horrible reservations who lived with hunger every day?" What will be your answer?

Sacred Sites

The first native people to occupy this country referred to it as Turtle Island and were a race now called Indians. The name was given to them by the first explorers who landed on these shores.

These Indians had many different beliefs than the white Europeans. This earth was their mother and no harm ever came to it during their existence. They believed in a higher power they referred to as *The Great Spirit* or *the Creator*. They looked to this Great Spirit for guidance in everything they did. They loved this country that He had blessed them with and for that reason it was sacred ground to them. They also believed that all living things were related to each other.

They were a family loving type of people; family and happiness were the two most important things in their lives. They believed that the Creator gave them everything they needed to have a good life. They never had nor needed money.

Indians were not lazy as the white race made them out to be. They did some amazing things on this earth. Many things they did will stand forever like the Great Indian Mounds that took hundreds of years to build by moving tons of dirt one basket at a time. Can you imagine the white race building a mound like the Indians did?

The Indian mounds were very special and sacred to the ones who made them and are still sacred to Indians today. It's just too bad that they were nothing to the white race that destroyed many of them. Many were burial sites. How would you like for the Indians to dig in your graveyards looking for relics?

All these mounds have special meanings of great importance. Even the Bible tells about these mounds in Proverbs 22:28 "Do not remove the ancient landmarks which your fathers have set." Many good Christians never see things like this in their Bibles.

Every mound ever made by Indians had some kind of special meaning. That doesn't matter to the majority of people living here today. No Indian mound is going to stand in the way of progress to money hungry vultures.

The day is coming when God will put Indian people back in charge of this country because they were the only ones that treated this earth like the Creator intended for all people to do.

What if they decided to put all white people on a reservation? It wouldn't be so funny then, would it?

My advice to the white race is to never destroy another Indian mound because the Creator sees everything you do and one day you will have to pay for your wrong doings. I love the Indian people and will do everything possible to help them and yes, I pay my tithes but not to the church. I pay them to help feed the hungry and support some of their schools on the reservations.

Trying to Make Sense of it All

Sometimes I am as confused as a new rooster in a hen house full of old turkey hens, not knowing which way to turn or what's going on in this crazy world.

Back when gasoline prices began to go up, retailers laid the blame on the cost of fuel for their price increases. Now that gasoline prices are dropping, you would think that everything else would be doing the same. Not so. Everything else just keeps going up. Is this good business or is it greed?

The owners of big businesses must think the working people are a bunch of dummies, and we are to some extent, because we just keep on paying their outrageous prices without complaining.

The cost of living goes up every year. People living on Social Security have not had a raise in years. The reason we don't get a raise is because our government has stolen our money from Social Security and now its going broke.

The vultures or buzzards in Washington see that money as a dead carcass. They flock to it and gobble it up until it's all gone. You can bet, if they ever get their hands in the pot where money is they won't leave until it's all gone.

Will American people ever learn to stop electing liars for office in our government? Maybe Americans just love liars.

Our government borrows money from China and probably other countries to keep our country operating. Then they turn around and give billions of dollars away every year to about 150 other countries This doesn't make a lick of sense to me. I don't believe there is a single tax payer who would agree with this. These jerks in Washington are supposed to be working for us, not against us. This country is almost ready to go down the drain. Will we sink before we can elect people that care about our country?

Out of all the politicians running for the highest office this year, how can we judge which one will make a good president? We can't go by what they say, because most of them are just saying what they think we want to hear; even if it is a lie.

The President we have wants to down size our military and has. That is one of the stupidest things I have ever heard from a Commander in Chief. It's just an invitation for other countries to invade us. Having a strong military is the one thing that keeps our freedom. Another thing he wants to do is take our guns away from law abiding citizens. If you think this is a good idea, just look at what happened to the Indians when the government took their guns.

Maybe the President doesn't want us to have guns so that we can't fight back when we get invaded by another country.

The Human Race

When you get right down to the bare facts, there is only one race on this earth and that is the human race. No matter what color your skin is or what country you are from, you belong to the human race. If all people could look at one another with this belief in their hearts, just think how much better off this world could be.

God didn't wake up one morning and say, "Today I will make the white man." He saw right off that man needed a mate. He said to Adam "I am going to make you a partner but it's going to hurt", so He snatched one of his ribs and made him a woman. The next day He made the black man and did the same for him, then the red and the yellow man. Now this is what a lot of people would like to believe and many do.

When God laid the laws down for us to follow and obey, He didn't have separate laws for each color of skin. God sees only one race and that is the human race. The problem with the human race is that all people have different beliefs about most everything and maybe that's God's intention.

He also gave us a choice to become whatever we choose to become. We can be a good person or we can be the devil in disguise. He also gives us guidelines for the way He wants us to live and go by.

We can become a very smart person because God gave us that ability. But no matter how educated and smart we become, we are still a first grader compared to the knowledge of our Creator. He knows all and if we follow His directions we will never go wrong.

People in this world are becoming so educated and smart that many believe that they are smarter and know more than this old-fashioned God of today.

It is a sad situation the way many believe. There are many in church every time the doors are open and call themselves Christians while still looking at other races as being unequal.

God made one man and one woman and that was the beginning of human life on this earth. Why are some of your relatives a different color? I have thought about this a lot. Maybe God just wanted to see our reaction when we see a person of a different color. Maybe it's just a test for Him to see what kind of person we really are.

It would be a wonderful life if everyone did what God wants them to do. We may be a rich man or we may be a poor man. No matter how much we think we own or how little, when it gets right down to it, we don't own a thing. It all belongs to God the Creator. He is just letting us use it for a short time.

The next time you see a black, red, yellow, brown or white person don't turn your nose up at them. Just speak and ask them how they're doing. Just remember God is watching and listening. Besides, you will feel a lot better if you show a little kindness to your relatives.

A Christian Nation

It is a very sad situation for this country to have the attitude it has about it being a Christian nation. It's easy for those living here today to ignore past history of this land. Maybe one of the easiest things one can do is to claim they are a Christian.

Have they ever looked back at the history of the newcomers who came into the country claiming to be Christians though that never stopped them from killing native people and taking their land? Now their comments about this are usually that "it was our ancestors; we had nothing to do with it."

The Indians your ancestors put on horrible reservations still live in the worst conditions of anyone here with many children going hungry and sleeping without adequate heat during cold winter months. Now, is that your ancestors' problem or maybe the blame falls on you.

A Christian nation lacks something when it won't help feed its poor. Some Christians will not lift a hand to help a brother or sister but make no mistake; Indian people are your brothers and sisters in God's eyes.

Where were all the good Christian people when one woman was responsible for taking God and prayer from our schools? Who stood up for God the Creator then? Even today so called Christians stand by and let our government do many ungodly things without protest. Television has become so filthy that it's not fit for animals to watch yet people rush home from church to turn it on.

Many things go on that make me think this is no longer a Christian nation. Killing and robbing are on a rampage and getting worse by the day. It has reached the point that it isn't even safe to leave home any more.

If you go to church on Sunday, the members eat you up with kindness but the next week they won't even know you. Is that the Christian way? Is it God's way for churches to look down on other churches? Is it right for one church to believe they are the only way to get to heaven? It wasn't a church that saved my soul; it was the grace of God. Too many so-called Christians have two personalities; their Sunday one and their every other day of the week one.

154

The first Indian schools started by whites were nothing more than horrible institutions where children were molested both sexually and physically by so called Christians. The punishment on the children was inhumane; they were forbidden to speak their own language and if they did they were made to eat soap. This happened in all the church related Indian schools and still happens in some churches today.

Preachers like to preach that the end of time is coming very soon. They can preach for hours on the subject, "Be ready today because tomorrow may be too late," but the next Sunday he will ask for money to build a new church because the one up the road is much better than ours and we need to outdo them. Makes one wonder why a new church is needed if the end is so near.

In most churches, the members are good people trying to do what is right. Churches are like all other groups; there are always some bad ones and they are the ones who keep a lot of people from going to church.

Whether you go to church or not, we all need to live by God's rules. His way is the only way because we live on His earth and He has the power to do anything He wants. I don't believe He likes what is happening on His earth today and if we don't soon put Him back at the head of the table, including our schools, government, homes and daily lives—He may give up on us.

Andrew Jackson – White People's Beloved President

Andrew Jackson was a very intelligent and great person according to white men's standards. He was very smart to make it all the way to the office of President of the United States.

It was President Thomas Jefferson who actually began the process of the Indian Removal Act but Andrew Jackson was the driving force behind it.

The Five Civilized Tribes of the Southeastern United States consisted of the Cherokee, Choctaw, Chickasaw, Creek and Seminole

Tribes. Andrew Jackson, through lies and false promises, had those tribes fighting with each other. One good example of this is when he had the Battle of Horseshoe Bend where the Choctaw, Chickasaw and many of the Creek Nation fought with him and his army against the Creeks, known as the Red Sticks.

Following many hours of hand to hand combat, the Red Sticks were defeated and the power and resistance of the Creek Nation was destroyed.

Instead of rewarding the Creeks who fought with him against the Creek Red Sticks, Andrew Jackson forced them to give up twenty two million acres of their land to the government. This is the kind of thanks Indian people usually received.

Known as a great hero to his kind, Jackson has been given credit for killing many Indian men, women and children. He loved doing what his race believed was a great and noble deed while thousands of Indians lost their lives from the actions of this killer.

One day on the battlefield, when he and his men thought they had killed all the Indians, there was one baby boy still alive. Jackson did take this boy home and raised him as his own. The boy's name was Lincoya who died at age sixteen. Andrew Jackson was campaigning for president at that time.

Jackson was honored greatly by the United States government with his picture and name placed on our twenty dollar bill. History books portray him as a great American hero.

In 1829 Jackson made a speech to some Indian people and it went like this:

"Friends and Brothers, by permission of the Great Spirit above, and the voice of the people, I have been made President of the United States, and now speak to you as your Father and Friend, and request you listen. Your warriors have known me long. You know I love my white and red children and always speak with a straight and not with a forked tongue; that I have always told you the truth. Where you now are; you and my white children are too near to each other to live in harmony and peace. Your game is destroyed and many of your people will not work and till the earth. Beyond the Great River Mississippi, where a part of your nation has gone, your Father has provided a country large enough for all of you and he advises you to remove to it. There your white brothers will not trouble you; they will have no claim to the land and you can live upon it, you and all your children, as long as the grass grows or the water flows, in peace and plenty and yours forever."

That was quite a speech for a person who had killed so many of the people he was talking to. The cruelest act in American history was carried out by this man and that was the *Trail of Tears.* Estimates are that about four thousand died on that march but if you count those who died in holding pens or stockades before the march began, the number would be much higher. But so what! They have always been considered less than human in this Christian nation.

Pharmaceutical Companies – Friend or Enemy?

About half the commercials on television today are from pharmaceutical companies. They advertise and push new medicines they so freely come out with. Then we have all the lawyers and law firms coming out with advertisements that "if you have taken some of those drugs, call us; you might be entitled to a large sum of money if you were harmed or killed by these drugs."

The drug companies know they are harmful to our bodies and could kill us but they make so much money off their poisons that they can put millions of dollars aside to take care of the lawsuits that will come and still make tons of money.

The people who watch these advertisements think that's just what they need to take and their doctors will oblige because they can make money, too. Most people must never hear about the side effects, but they are sometimes worse than the problem the medications treat.

Webster's Dictionary, printed in 1980, defines the word 'pharmaceutical' as the practice of witchcraft or the use of poisons. Now that is quite a statement but true. It amazes me the amount of drugs people now take every day, especially older people.

Every pill made by pharmaceutical companies is poison to our bodies. At the top of the list as being most dangerous is chemotherapy. It has probably killed more people than the cancer it is used to treat.

While many older people look down on the younger generation for doing drugs, which is very wrong and has become epidemic many of them are just as much an addict as the young. However, because they get theirs from doctors, they think it's alright.

Many Christian people think they can do no wrong; they study the Bible and are in church every time the doors are open but then take a handful of pills every day. They want to tell others what they are doing wrong but don't even realize that taking that handful of pills went against what the Bible teaches. God does not want us to take poisons that harm our bodies and you can be assured that these pills are poison.

Would someone tell me where in the Bible it says that medicine is supposed to be made of synthetic materials? He tells us where to get our medicine for healing and it is not from a laboratory where a bunch of scientists work with all sorts of poisons.

Here is a warning from Thomas Jefferson: "If people let the government decide what foods they can eat and what medicines they can take, their bodies will soon be in as sorry a state as are the souls of those who live under tyranny." The Bible tells us that medicine is good and where to obtain it, from herbs.

Cancer research has been under way for years without much progress. A ton of money has been given to find a cure but personally, they will never find one using poison chemicals. There are cures for most diseases, but they are not from poisonous medicine but from herbs. Our government will never let this be known because they want people to die off. There will never be a cure for cancer or other diseases as long as we have a government like ours.

Most people have looked down on Indians but they are the only ones who did what the Creator expected all to do. Their medicines are from herbs. They love all things created by the Great Spirit and never needed a Bible to teach them what was right.

Lord help us now. Just look at what these foreigners have done to what was once a paradise.

I Do what My God wants Me to Do

Having nothing against any of the churches in our community, I would be attending if not for one reason; they expect us to give our tithes, sometimes more, and make us feel obligated to do so. God laid something on my heart years ago and to me there is nothing more important that what He says in *Proverbs 21:13*, "Whoever shuts his ears to the cry of the poor will also cry himself and not be heard."

Having heard the cry of the poor from the Indian reservations out west, I promised God to do everything possible to help my brothers and sisters. This is something I will do for the rest of my life because this is what's important and what God wants me to do.

God gave me the ability to love all people regardless the color of their skin or their religious affiliation. There is no hate in my heart for anyone.

But there is one thing I have never been able to understand. Why do none of the churches want to talk about the Native American Indians? To me they were the only race that did everything according to God's will. Could it be that our ancestors came into this country killing them and stealing their land while calling themselves Christians and we are ashamed and don't want to talk about it?

God knows everything that happened to the Indians and He knows how badly they are still treated. Now I wonder who He is angry with; the foreigners who did the killing back then are not the only ones that will be held accountable. Many people today will be accountable for the way they are still being treated.

To me, the Indians were God's greatest race, free from all diseases. He gave them a paradise to live upon; they used herbs for medicine like God said to do; they never had nor needed money to live and be happy. That had to be God's way of life.

They were good people who prayed about everything before doing anything. They knew there was a higher power leading them. Even when they killed an animal for food, a prayer was offered up to the Creator. They had never seen nor heard of the Bible. God gave the white people the Bible to go by and they still cannot get things right.

Maybe if some of the preachers that live so high and mighty would take a trip to a place like Pine Ridge Reservation, drive through it and stop to see how they live in those shacks. Visit with some of the hungry children, and then they could get a feel of how they have to live. Maybe then they could see that those fancy churches they preach in could be just a little smaller.

Please remember that the land our homes and churches sit upon and all the other lands were stolen from the Indians. It is my belief that God would be overjoyed if the people in this country gave some of it back to the rightful owners, but that will never happen because of white man's greed. Greed is a disease that has taken over our country and the churches are not immune to it.

What Goes Around Comes Around

"What goes around comes around' is an old saying that has a lot of truth in it. We are in a terrible mess in our great country today. You might say that war has come to our homeland. Many bad things are happening that we never dreamed of years ago. There are mass killings every few weeks; individuals are stealing, killing and robbing every day. The time is drawing near when you will be in danger every time you leave home.

Why are things getting so bad now? There are many reasons and I believe one of the main ones is that people are turning away from God the Creator. I could tell you that the invention of computers with the internet is one, but who would believe that? I ask you why not? They have opened up all countries information to the whole world.

The elected officials we have in our government today act like they are against the American way of life. It looks like some of them don't even care about right anymore. I believe some of them are better qualified to be in the cotton fields picking cotton.

There doesn't seem to be love for our country anymore. The love of money, wealth, power and lust has replaced that love. The television that you enjoy watching so much is a bad omen. It is good at programming your mind that bad is good.

I know the people living in this country today had nothing to do with the massacre of the Indian people, but your ancestors did. There are many Indians still on the white man's reservations living in poverty. They didn't ask for this. They were forced into it. Did they deserve this? No, they did not. This was their country that they love very much.

I don't think the people living in this country today think they have any obligation at all to the Indian people. It may not be about what you think, but about what God thinks.

Most of those living in this country today have done nothing to correct what your ancestors did to the Native people. I guess you think that God thinks it's all right for His people to go hungry and cold on these reservations.

I believe that some of you think you are God's greatest gift to society and the superior race of this world. I'm sure it would be interesting to know what God thinks about you.

Could it be time for what goes around to come back around? Remember when your ancestors came into this country killing the Native people and stealing this land? I hope that people of today don't think that God can just forget about what happened back then to some of His beloved people.

If the people of today along with the government had just tried to make amends to the Indians and helped them get back on their feet and if they could have received what the government had promised, things just might be a little different now. That never happened, so what is happening in our country today just might be payback time.

It is a horrible thing that the terrorists are doing today and I don't know if our government knows what to do about it. They are good about talking about it, but that's all.

Most people think that the terrorist attacks are the worst thing that has ever happened in America. But it is not. It would be hard to describe what your ancestors did to the Native American Indians. My God knows and has all the answers to all problems. And I pray that you will never have to go through what my Indian people had to go through.

161

The Wise Old Indian

If you ride through or are close to one of the Indian reservations out west and see an old Indian wandering around like he might be lost, hair that looks as if it hasn't seen a comb in a month of Sundays, wearing rags on his back and looking like he hasn't had a bath in a while, don't be too quick to judge the old rogue.

Many old Indians can tell you more about what's going to happen in the future than some of the most brilliant minds in the country. It may be that the Creator put the ability into the old codger's brain or maybe he had visions shown to him about what's going to happen. I would believe his words and trust his knowledge more than some of the foreign geniuses.

Having never met a dumb old Indian, I am amazed at the knowledge they have about all things pertaining to life in general. Believe me; they will be glad to tell you what's going to happen in the future of this country. Most of you might not want to hear but I would bet money you can sit back and see them come true.

If the foreigners here really want to know what is going to happen to our country and the people you can find out by listening to a group of old Indians sitting around a campfire talking to one another.

Before white men came here, the Indians lived a life pleasing to the Creator; for that reason they never needed a Bible. They lived a life white men could never comprehend. Can you just imagine a white man living without money or greed in their heart, without hate and all those high-tech gadgets?

Indians had no schools so the elders taught the children everything they needed to know in order to live a good and happy life. One could say the elders were outstanding teachers and their pay scale was zero. Indian people did almost everything out of love for their own.

Elders have tons of knowledge stored up in their minds; if they need to know something else, they talk to the Creator and wait for an answer that always comes. They were highly respected and looked up to with much honor in their tribe. Their advice was always taken on important decisions concerning the tribe and they were not put into old folks homes like people today. Indians love their old people too much to

162

do that. It seems like today people can't wait to truck their old folks off to those homes and sometimes I think, "What else can you expect from the white race?"

Indians never had hospitals because there was no need. They had medicine men and women to take care of minor problems. They had no jails because the elders decided on the punishment to be applied to the wrong doer. Things moved at a slower pace when only the Indians occupied this land. If they traveled it was by foot, horse or canoe.

The elders have many stories about many different things they passed down to the children, who were always eager to listen. Many of the old stories have now vanished and been forgotten because some of the children picked up on the white man's ways. They no longer want to listen to their elders. If you live among corruption, sooner or later you will become corrupt.

Saving Native Horses and Helping Native People

Sometimes you get to know some outstanding people who do some amazing things with their lives. It was a great honor for me to meet a family of this caliber a few years back. Their names are Sean and Yvette Collin. They had two children of their own at the time, Huyanha and Cruz. Later Yvette gave birth to a boy named Nakota Braveheart.

The Collins moved from California to Florence, Alabama because Sean was engaged in legal work in Florence. On one of his trips, he brought Yvette with him and she fell in love with the area. She told him, "This is where we are going to live and raise our family."

They bought a farm outside the City of Florence and began their great work with horses and people. They are family oriented, including their children as much as possible in their endeavors. Sean had two adopted children before he and Yvette married; their names are James and Amelia.

Sean is of Cherokee and Euchee while Yvette is Cheyenne, Arapaho, Comanche and Mayan on her mother's side and Natoka, Choctaw or Cherokee on her father's side.

Sean owns a business in Florence, teaches at UNA (University of North Alabama), and practices law. Yvette is a doctoral candidate and fellow at the University of Alaska, Fairbanks. She has a BA from Johns Hopkins (writing seminars) and a joint MA from New York University (Journalism and Latin American Caribbean Studies). She is an award winning journalist and has held various executive positions at non-profit institutions around the U. S. She practices her people's traditional ways and strives each day to follow in the footsteps of her ancestors.

Yvette and Sean founded Sacred Way Sanctuary (*www.sacredwaysanctuary.org*) which is located in Florence. They have spent years tracing both oral history and spiritual practices of many Native American peoples with regard to their traditional horses and gathering representatives of what is left of these endangered creatures for preservation.

Yvette, through research and study, has proven that horses were here in this nation long before any Spanish people arrived on our shores bringing with them some horses. Many times the native horse was called a Spanish horse. The history of this country is flawed greatly by the first intruders because of their dislike for the natives.

Mrs. Collin has lectured throughout the U. S. on these subjects as well as in China and Vietnam. The *Spirit Horse Medicine Way* was first presented at the World Indigenous Peoples Conference on Education in Hawaii in May, 2014. Both Yvette and Sean gave speeches at this gathering.

Sean spends the week working at his job and on the weekends he works at their farm. They have about 150 native horses, four brown and one white buffalo, along with some four-horned Navajo sheep, goats, chickens, ducks, other fowl, and a rare breed of dogs. Yvette spends every day all day feeding all the animals. She has some help but does most of the work herself.

They have a sweat lodge on their property that is used often. She also has a large tee pee where she holds meeting with women and teaches them the spiritual ways of Native Indians.

The reason they have so many native horses, especially Cherokee and Choctaw, is because they heard they were going to kill them if someone didn't take them. They were not going to allow this breed to become extinct so they travelled to Oklahoma and brought truckloads of them back to their farm.

They help with the Sun Dance every year in the Black Hills of South Dakota on the Wild Horse Sanctuary. This is a very spiritual event, held around the middle of June. In 2013, Yvette danced every dance for four days while fasting for the duration and gave birth to a baby boy on August 29th that summer. A midwife delivered the baby in a tee pee on their farm. He was named Nakota Braveheart and I received the greatest honor of becoming his godfather.

You would think they would not have time to do anything else yet this couple travels near and far helping Native people. They pray for them and with them and do whatever is necessary to help them. They often travel to many of the reservations to talk, pray and help people any way they can and would never take monetary help for what they do. They do not believe in taking anything for doing the Creator's work. Most everything they do is connected to the Creator. They are probably known by more Native Indians than any other family because of the amount of work they do for them.

You may not read about them in the newspaper or magazines or see them on television because that is not what they are all about. Their reward and recognition will come in their next life. I have been on this earth for 84 years and in all my days I have never met any as spiritual as this family. Anytime you are around them you can feel the presence of the Great Spirit.

They took me in and made me part of their family and I love them as my own. Being a godfather to Nakota and a Grandpa to Huyanha and Cruz is a gift from heaven for this old man.

I believe it is time for them to get some recognition for all they do and if there is anyone who works harder than them to save the endangered native horses or their traditional way of life, I have yet to meet them.

It would be very hard to list all they do for others and animals. They are very dedicated to everything they do. You could say that Yvette is a walking miracle to come from a very bad life, not by her own fault by any means. The life she now leads bubbles over with enthusiasm and she credits the Creator and her horses for that.

Some words from Yvette:

"The world is beginning to understand that there is something special between horse and mankind, and that it is not just that the animal can be physically and economically useful. Today there are many children, youth, veterans and others in need of healing who are benefiting from being able to spend time with these creatures in a safe and loving environment. In an attempt to measure and record, western science is now endeavoring to understand what it is about the 'horse and man' combination that is enabling certain patients to move forward when other more mainstream treatments have failed.

"Although most Native American cultures did not feel the need to understand everything about the Great Mystery (Creator) and they did not seek, feel the need or see the value in measuring and recording in the same manner as western science, these tribes had thousands of years during which to perfect their spiritual and healthcare practices. They knew what worked and how to replicate the conditions for it to reoccur.

"Personally, I am eternally grateful for the gift of 'Spirit Horse Medicine' for a time in my life when I needed it most and was deemed incurable by western science, the wisdom of my ancestors came through for me. Like my Cheyenne, Nakota and Mayan ancestors and many other native peoples before me, I was able to receive spiritual, mental, emotional and physical healing to a level that modern medicine believed to be impossible. This miracle was through the love of a creature that much of the world still believes to be little more than property."

A Native American Prayer

O Great Spirit, Creator of all life, I come to you with
much sadness in my heart. My people have always praised
You and looked to You for guidance in everything we do. I
beg for understanding for the mistreatment of my
ancestors and their way of life.
Why did another race of people land on the shores of our homelands
and disrupt our way of life?
Why did they introduce us to a drink that my people could not
tolerate, by trading their whiskey for our beautiful furs?
Why did they bring their sicknesses and diseases into our country?
It was a sickness that killed thousands of my people, as they had no
immunities against these diseases.
Why did they bring the long guns and kill the wild animals? This
was our main source of food, why did they kill just for the pure
pleasure of killing?
Why were there so many, enough to force us from our homes and
overpower and kill most of my people?
Why did they take everything from us, even give us a number and
take away our names?
Why did the U. S. Government make so many treaties with my
people; then break every one of them?

Why did they take our homes, our animals and all our belongings?
Then, they forced us to reservations on lands that were worthless to
them.
Why do some still have to live on these reservations with living
conditions well below the poverty level? We are cold in the
wintertime, hot in the summertime; we are always hungry and
sickness rages.
Lord, we search our hearts for answers, but find none. We lift our
hands up to You in prayer because You are the One that will take
our souls to the Spirit World. We were a beaten down people but we
have always held onto our faith in You.

Marty, Willene, & Dale Casteel

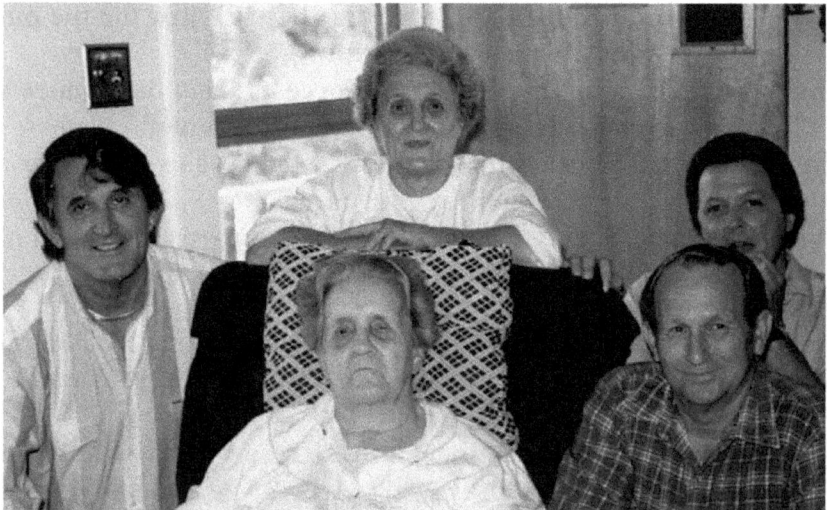

**Back: Dale, Marion and Billy
Front: Mom and Jimmy Casteel**

1948-1949 Basketball Team
L – R: Rex White, Edward Briddges, William McElyea, Benton
Ball & Dale Casteel

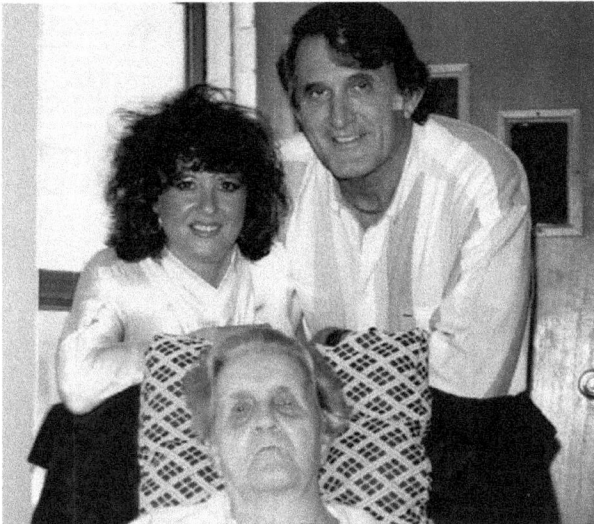

Jo & Dale Casteel with Mom

Tom Cook, Arena Director
Of the Sun Dance

Back: Marty & Liz
Front: Dale & Anna

ANNIE MOORE HANEY
A Native American
I'm Honor'd to be your
Great Grandson
Dale Casteel

Grave Marker for Annie Moore Haney

Bluewater Publications is a multi-faceted publishing company capable of meeting all of your reading and publishing needs. Our two-fold aim is to:

1) Provide the market with educationally enlightening and inspiring research and reading materials.

2) Make the opportunity of being published available to any writer and/or researcher who desires to be published.

We are passionate about preserving history; whether through the re-publishing of an out-of-print classic, or by publishing the research of historians and genealogists. Bluewater Publications is the Peoples' Choice Publisher.

For company information or information about how you can be published through Bluewater Publications, please visit:

www.BluewaterPublications.com

Also check Amazon.com to purchase any of the books that we publish.

Confidently Preserving Our Past,

Bluewater Publications.com

www.ingramcontent.com/pod-product-compliance
Lightning Source LLC
Chambersburg PA
CBHW070758100426
42742CB00012B/2178